RICHARD TILL

TO MY MOTHER

First published in 2008 by
Renaissance Publishing, Auckland
PO Box 36 206, Northcote
Auckland
rl@renaissancepublishing.co.nz

10 9 8 7 6 5 4 3 2

ISBN: 978-0-9582635-6-6

A catalogue record for this book is available
from the National Library of New Zealand

Design: Trevor Newman
Editor: Alison Dench

Printed by Spectrum Print

CONTENTS

Introduction

KIWI KITCHEN CELEBRATES THE EVERYDAY CREATIONS OF THE HOME COOKS OF NEW ZEALAND. IT'S A COLLECTION OF THE RECIPES DEMONSTRATED TO ME BY THE DOZENS OF ORDINARY AND EXTRAORDINARY PEOPLE WE VISITED IN SERIES TWO — FOLLOWED IN EACH CHAPTER BY A MENU OF MY OWN RECIPES INSPIRED BY THE THEME OR LOCATION OF EACH EPISODE.

IN THE END, IT'S REALLY ABOUT THE FOOD OUR MOTHERS MADE FOR US AND THE RECIPES AND TRADITIONS THEY HAVE HANDED DOWN. OPENING THE BACK DOOR OF THE FAMILY HOME TO BE GREETED BY THE DELIGHTFUL SMELL OF A ROAST IN THE OVEN IS HEART-WARMING IN THE EXTREME. THE TANTALISING AROMA OF A MEAL COOKING IS ONE OF THE WAYS WE EXTEND THE PLEASURE OF FOOD INTO THE HOURS BEFORE IT ARRIVES.

HOUSES SHOULD REGULARLY BE FILLED WITH THE AROMA OF A MEAL UNDER CONSTRUCTION. IT'S MY GREATEST HOPE THAT THE RECIPES IN THIS BOOK WARM HEARTS, GET FAMILIES AROUND THE TABLE TOGETHER AND GIVE ENCOURAGEMENT TO EVERY MEMBER OF THE HOUSEHOLD TO DEVELOP THEIR SKILLS IN THE KITCHEN. THE RECIPES ARE TRIED AND TESTED, OFTEN OVER GENERATIONS, AND COVER A WIDE RANGE OF METHODS AND STYLES OF COOKERY. WHEN YOU MAKE THEM, KEEP A CLOSE EYE ON WHAT IS GOING ON IN THE POT, PAN OR ROASTING TIN AND TRUST YOUR INTUITION ABOUT WHERE YOU CAN APPLY THE METHODS TO OTHER DISHES YOU MIGHT ASPIRE TO MAKE.

IT'S EASY TO BE INTIMIDATED BY THE EFFORTS OF THE COOKING PROFESSIONALS AND THE COMPLEX INSTRUCTIONS THEY SOMETIMES GIVE. BUT COOKING IS NOT THAT DIFFICULT WHEN ALL IS SAID AND DONE. THE KEY ATTRIBUTES OF SUCCESSFUL COOKERY ARE ENTHUSIASM FOR THE TASKS INVOLVED, AND A SENSE OF LOVE AND CARE FOR THE INGREDIENTS — AND FOR THOSE FOR WHOM YOU ARE COOKING.

Cans of fancy pink salmon were the cornerstone of my mother's fancy catering in flash meals. I spent a fair amount of time in my teenage years trying to catch salmon and never succeeding, so I'm well placed to believe that an average salmon fisherman's yearly catch is zero.

Mum's Place
Waitaki

Most families have favourite dishes called 'mum's' this, or 'nana's' that. My family is no exception. Sadly, my mother died before the first series of *Kiwi Kitchen* was screened but of course her culinary influence is still with me, which is one of the reasons we filmed the first episode of the second series in and around Oamaru, her home town.

In my mother's case canned salmon was an indicator of 'fancy' in cooking (it actually had the words 'fancy pink salmon' on the label!). Canned salmon was powerfully versatile when she made luncheon for guests, appearing in three ways: 'fast and fancy', i.e., turned straight out of the can into the middle of arranged salad items; 'a lot of effort fancy' as moulded salmon mousse; and 'perilous fancy' as salmon soufflé, which was my favourite by far. I was a pushy teenage kitchen assistant, always wanting to make a salmon soufflé for fancy lunches.

My mother's stamping ground of Oamaru is utopia for new potatoes. Little boxes of Jersey Bennes travel to every corner of the country and are recognised as true new potatoes. Personally, I don't think it's possible to have Christmas without the twin delights of new potatoes and just-picked peas.

The Waitaki River, not so far from Oamaru, is big in South Island salmon. There are a great many salmon-fishing enthusiasts in small villages around the river mouth, among them Geoff and Pat Vause. Their shelves are full of home-bottled fish, some of which dates back several seasons (vintage fish, anyone?). Pat led us through the preserving process, then whipped up some of her bottled salmon into a baked mornay dish. Nowadays we've become so accustomed to salmon as farmed fish, smoked and fresh, that a can or a bottle of salmon offers an unfamiliar, delicious savoury experience.

Pat's Salmon Mornay

Pat's savoury bake is a homely kitchen-table version of crayfish mornay, in which the fish and sauce become one as the dish cooks. By the way, mornay sauce is really just white sauce with cheese, sometimes sharpened with a little mustard.

15 g butter
2 Tbsp flour
1½ cups milk
1 tsp chicken stock powder
½ cup grated mild cheese
1 tsp lemon juice
chopped fresh parsley to taste
1 x 210 g can salmon, drained
1 tomato, finely sliced
1 hard-boiled egg, peeled and
    finely sliced
dry breadcrumbs and extra
    grated cheese for topping

Preheat the oven to 180°C.

Melt butter in a saucepan. Add flour. Cook a little then, with the pan still over the heat, slowly add milk, beating with a wooden spoon until it's a nice smooth mixture. Remove from heat and add stock powder, cheese, lemon juice and parsley.

Flake salmon into an ovenproof dish. Pour sauce over flaked salmon. Arrange slices of tomato and egg on top. Sprinkle with breadcrumbs and a little more cheese.

Bake for about 35 minutes until bubbling and golden.

SERVES 4

Sue's Apricot-Glazed Ham

Fresh new potatoes go perfectly with a slice of ham. Sue Smith gave the ham an extra layer of flavour with a simple yet nifty glaze.

cooked ham on the bone, skin removed
handful of whole cloves
1 cup apricot jam
2 tsp mustard powder
1 Tbsp soy sauce

Preheat the oven to 200°C.

Place ham in a baking dish. Score fat with a diamond pattern (if that's your thing), then push in the cloves to match the pattern.

Mix together the jam, mustard and soy sauce. Brush over the ham and bake for 30-45 minutes, basting regularly until the fat and glaze caramelise deliciously.

NEW POTATOES ARE JUST ABOUT THE ONLY TRULY SEASONAL VEGETABLE LEFT THESE DAYS. THEY TRY TO FLOG US IMPORTED ASPARAGUS OUT OF SEASON, BUT I'VE YET TO RUN ACROSS NEW POTATOES FLOWN IN FROM SOMEONE ELSE'S LATE SPRING. SOME RESTAURANTS TRY TO PASS OFF THOSE LITTLE GOURMET POTATOES AS IF THEY WERE NEW, BUT THE REAL THING IS SOMETHING WORTH STAYING TRUE TO.

As farmers of a big chunk of the best potato-growing (and cricket pitch) soil in the country Sue and Lindsay Smith served us a beautiful lunch of new Red Kings and Jersey Bennes that were so fresh you could blow the skins off. Alongside them was a ham that had come from a member of the family operating a piggery with generous animal welfare practices on the other side of State Highway 1.

June's Trifle

June made the sponge, from the recipe on the Fielder's Cornflour packet, three or four days before making the trifle. You could also use a bought sponge – just leave it on the bench to dry out a bit.

2 Tbsp custard powder
3 cups milk
raspberry jam for spreading
1 sponge cake, 3–4 days old
1 x 410 g can peaches in syrup
⅓ cup sherry
nip of whisky
2 Tbsp sugar
250 ml cream
strawberries to decorate

Combine the custard powder with the milk according to the directions on the packet and allow to cool.

Spread the jam over the sponge, then cut it into 2 cm squares. Put the sponge squares into the serving bowl.

Mix together the syrup from the peaches, the sherry and the whisky. Pour this liquid over the sponge. Cut up the peaches and put them on top of the sponge. Pour the cool custard into the bowl to cover the peaches and soaked sponge squares.

Cover and refrigerate for at least 6 hours.

Before serving, add the sugar to the cream, whip and spoon onto the top of the trifle. Decorate with the strawberries.

SERVES 6

Up the Waitaki Valley at Kurow, where I holidayed in my childhood, the *Kiwi Kitchen* team visited June Taylor. She had inherited the most amazing piece of Dr Seuss-ish topiary when she retired here. The topiary on its own seemed worth the trip, but the real point was to try June's trifle. She had recently been handed the mantle of official family trifle maker. Not a role to be taken lightly.

RICHARD'S EASY ENTERTAINING MENU

Cheap tricks with supermarket products that can add to your dinner party repertoire and a dessert inspired by Joy Bars and Jelly Tips.

Salmon on Potato Cake

This quick-to-prepare entrée is surely one of the easiest ways to look like you went to a lot of delicious trouble, when you actually just went shopping. I prefer using round hash browns, and hot smoked salmon rather than cold.

    frozen hash browns, at least 2 per person
    cream cheese
    smoked salmon
    dressing (see recipe below)
    fresh herbs to garnish

Grill, bake or fry the hash browns according to your preference.
  Put two cooked hash browns in the centre of each serving plate, and top with a tablespoon of cream cheese. Pile a generous amount of smoked salmon on top of the cream cheese and spoon over some dressing.
  Choose herbs to garnish as your mood and sense of fashion dictates.

Dressing

An excellent all-purpose vinaigrette, this recipe will provide more than you are likely to need for this dish (unless you are having 30 people for dinner). It keeps very well in the fridge in a screw-top jar.

    2 Tbsp fresh mint
    1 cup extra virgin olive oil
    1/4 cup cider vinegar
    1/2 tsp salt
    1-2 cloves garlic, peeled
    1 Tbsp brown sugar
    1 tsp mustard

Put all the ingredients in a large bowl and whizz with a stick blender. Alternatively, blend or process in the appropriate machine. Or you could chop the mint and garlic by hand and mix everything together with a spoon.

ROAST POTATOES WHEN YOU AREN'T HAVING A ROAST — THESE HAVE TO BE SEEN AS GATEWAY FOOD FOR VEGETARIANS CURIOUS ABOUT THE PLEASURES OF MEAT JUICES. I'M CERTAIN THAT ONE BITE OF THE CRISP BROWN EXTERIOR WOULD MAKE SOME OF THEM RECONSIDER.

Potatoes Roasted with Stock

When you can't have new potatoes, there are plenty of fabulous ways to have main crop old potatoes and this is a sensationally good preparation (with more than a whisper of that wonderful old hotel style). I favour Agria potatoes but any spuds indicated as good for roasting will do. Also known as Chateau Potatoes, this is the traditional side dish for Chateaubriand.

1.5 kg medium-sized
   roasting potatoes
4 Tbsp vegetable oil
about 1300 ml beef stock

Preheat the oven (ideally fan forced) to 200°C.
  Peel the potatoes using a small knife, creating as many flat surfaces as possible – much like a faceted jewel. They brown better this way, plus they look delightfully old-fashioned. If you are preparing them ahead of time, keep them in cold water but dry them off before using.

  Heat a large roasting pan in the oven. Add the oil to the pan and return it to the oven for a few minutes until it is good and hot.

  Add the potatoes to the pan and cook, removing the pan every 10 minutes and giving it a good shake, for 30 minutes.

  Add the stock to the pan and cook (turning the potatoes from time to time) until all the stock has been absorbed. At this point the potatoes will be very nicely browned, tender and deliciously meaty.

  Serve with grilled meat and salad.

SERVES 6

Richard's Trifle

Even if, like me, you don't much care for trifle, you might find you like these individual desserts. Make them in glasses so you can tailor them to each diner (no booze for the children who don't like the taste, and double sherry for Nana, if that's her thing). Use home-made custard if you can be bothered making it.

3 regular punnets berry fruit
1 packet each raspberry and
　blackberry jelly crystals
1 supermarket chocolate sponge
1 litre ready-made custard
liquor of your choice
vanilla ice-cream
chocolate crackle ice-cream topping

Wash and trim the berry fruit, and chop up half of it. Put the chopped fruit in a shallow dish, reserving the whole fruit.

Make up jelly according to the instructions on the packet but using half the amount of boiling water. Tip the double-strength jelly liquid over the chopped fruit. Leave to set for 2–3 hours.

Cut the chocolate sponge into 2 cm squares.

It's best to prepare the ingredients up to the ice-cream and chocolate crackle topping stage, then assemble the trifles before serving the main course. This will allow time for the ice-cream to soften a little and start to run into the lower layers.

Start by pouring some custard into the bottom of each glass. Add some of the whole berry fruit followed by a layer of sponge squares. Add a nip of the liquor of your choice – or not. Top with broken-up jelly and finish with a mound of ice-cream covered with chocolate crackle topping.

MAKES 8–10 INDIVIDUAL TRIFLES

I THINK IT'S A GREAT IDEA TO MAKE THESE TRIFLES IN INDIVIDUAL GLASSES, NOT LEAST BECAUSE YOU CAN THEN TAILOR THEM TO EACH DINER

PICNICS HAVE EVOLVED THEIR OWN SUB-
CATEGORY OF FOOD. TO JOIN THIS CATEGORY – IN
MY OPINION, ANYWAY – A FOOD STUFF REALLY
NEEDS TO BE ROBUST AND, IF AT ALL POSSIBLE,
SQUARE OR RECTANGULAR. THINK SANDWICHES
CUT, STACKED AND WRAPPED INTO PARCELS,
RECTANGULAR PIE TINS, HUNKS OF FRUITCAKE.
HOWEVER, A SEPARATE PIE DISH IS ACCEPTABLE.

The Great Summer Picnic
Hawke's Bay

I though Hawke's Bay might be the picnic capital of New Zealand for the sun never stops shining there. So that's where we went to find a few picnickers.

Picnics were a commonplace part of my childhood, the natural accompaniment to a long car trip. For one thing there weren't cafés every 10 minutes along State Highway 1, and even if there had been it would have felt very indulgent to use them without significant cause. Our picnics took place in the domains of small towns or a few hundred metres down a dusty side road. A rug, wicker basket, tea from a Thermos, slightly soggy tomato sandwiches, baking from the tins — these were the defining features of a traveller's lunch.

Of course there were also special picnics, an event in themselves, in which the cricket bat got packed, togs for the beach, and the catering got more attention. Another Thermos with iced cordial, plus cold sausages and luxury sandwiches such as Marmite and potato-crisp. Same rug, same wicker, just an elevated sense of occasion.

I continued to picnic with my own children, but only the special occasion picnic survived. The wicker was still there, but it was filled with quiche, pizza, pasta salad and products straight from the supermarket. We still drove somewhere, but no longer did we sit two feet from the car, and if someone took a photo the car no longer made it into the shot.

These days the urge to picnic often takes us no further than our own patios — the antipasto platter on the recently renovated indoor/outdoor living area, with Sauvignon Blanc all round. It's not quite like old times.

Hester's Broad Beans and Peas with Mint and Feta

Hester describes this as 'a fresh tasting salad, ideal for the outdoors to eat with crusty French bread', which it surely is. It's somewhere between a dip, a pâté and a salad, and is absolutely delicious.

175 g frozen broad beans
500 g frozen minted peas
handful of cubed feta cheese
fresh red chilli to taste, finely chopped
large handful of roughly chopped mint
1–2 Tbsp extra virgin olive oil
freshly ground black pepper to taste

Bring a large pot of water to the boil. Add broad beans, then allow the water to come back to the boil. Remove beans with a slotted spoon to a colander and refresh under cold water. When they are cool, slip off the dull greenish grey skins to reveal the limey green beans inside and place these in a bowl.

Quickly blanch the minted peas and allow to cool. Process the peas with the broad beans to a rough lime-green purée.

Tip this into a bowl, add the feta cheese, chopped chilli and mint, olive oil and lots of black pepper. Taste and season further if necessary.

SERVES 8

HESTER GUY IS A VERY EXPERIENCED CATERER AND COOKING DEMONSTRATOR. SHE HAD HER OWN TELEVISION SERIES IN THE 1980s AND HER HESTER GUY SALADS, ALL READY TO GO FOR ANY PICNIC ANYWHERE, ANYTIME, WERE SOLD IN SUPERMARKETS NATIONWIDE. HESTER SHOWED US SEVERAL MODERN, STYLISH DISHES PERFECTLY ADAPTED FOR SUMMER PATIO LIVING AND EQUALLY EASILY PACKED IN THE WICKER FOR A WINERY CONCERT OR A DAY AT THE RACES.

Hester's Chicken, Grape and Almond Salad with Lemon and Herb Mayonnaise

This recipe uses chicken breasts but would also be a great way to flash-up a supermarket rotisserie chicken. Hester makes a beautiful lemon and herb mayonnaise, but you can store-bought mayonnaise and add the juice of a lemon or lime and a handful of chopped fresh herbs. The ingredients for the salad can be prepared in advance and kept covered in the fridge for up 24 hours, and assembled just before serving.

- 6 boneless, skinless chicken breasts,
    cooked and allowed to cool
- 4–6 stalks celery
- 400 g grapes (green or red)
- 3 spring onions
- 3–4 Tbsp sliced almonds
- 1 cup lemon and
    herb mayonnaise (see recipe opposite)

Slice the chicken against the grain on the diagonal. Peel the coarse string from the back of the celery and slice into thin diagonal strips. Halve grapes and remove the seeds. Finely slice the spring onions. Lightly toast the almonds in the oven.

   Assemble the salad by layering the ingredients (except for the almonds) with the herb mayo on a large platter. Scatter the almonds on top.

SERVES 12

Lemon and Herb Mayonnaise

This mayonnaise will keep in the fridge for about a week. Sometimes Hester thins it with a little boiling water or folds in a couple of tablespoons of plain yoghurt.

2 egg yolks
1 clove garlic, peeled (optional)
½ Tbsp mild mustard
rind of 1 lemon
1 Tbsp lemon juice
½ tsp salt
¼ tsp freshly ground black pepper
1 cup grapeseed oil (or canola oil)
1–2 Tbsp finely chopped chives
   or parsley

Place egg yolks, garlic, mustard, lemon rind and juice, salt and pepper in food processor and process together.

With food processor running, very slowly drizzle the oil through the feed tube. Gradually the yolks will combine with the oil to form a thick, rich, buttery mayonnaise. The oil must be combined with the egg yolk mixture very slowly initially, until you are certain an emulsion has formed and the mixture has not curdled. If your mayonnaise does curdle, cream an additional egg yolk very well and slowly drip it from a teaspoon into the curdled mixture until the oil combines with the yolk base.

Taste the mayonnaise for seasoning, adding extra lemon juice if necessary. Add the herbs.

MAKES 1 CUP

Graham's Bacon and Egg Pie

Graham King's rendering of the bacon and egg pie is very fine, the highlight being his immaculate pastry technique. I recommend his pastry as a fabulous all-purpose savoury pastry. Graham says you can add chives, spring onions and parsley to the bacon and egg if you want to, but I got the feeling this is a concession to fancy city folk who can't leave well enough alone. I know where he is coming from. Sometimes simple things are best as they are. Having said that, I'm partial to some tomato and peas in my bacon and egg pie. It's a South Island, south of the Rakaia thing.

2 cups flour
100 g butter, chopped into small pieces
50 g lard, chopped into small pieces
pinch of salt
1 dessertspoon lemon juice
cold water to mix
handful of grated cheese
500 g bacon
as many eggs as you need (somewhere between 6 and 10)
salt and pepper to taste
egg or milk for glaze

Sift flour into a bowl. Make a well in the centre and mix in butter and lard, salt and lemon juice. Rub in. Gradually add water to the mixture until you are able to roll it out with a rolling pin. Allow pastry dough to chill for an hour.

Preheat the oven as high as it can go on fan bake.

Roll out dough and use it to line a greased 20 cm tin, reserving some of the pastry for the lid. Sprinkle grated cheese in the bottom and add a layer of whole bacon rashers. Break eggs into the pie and break yolks with fork. Add more bacon, chopped, and salt and pepper. Top with pastry and glaze with egg or milk. Prick holes in pastry lid.

Place pie in hot oven, turn temperature down to 200°C and bake for 20–30 minutes.

SERVES 4–6

The very best picnics had a bacon and egg pie that had been baked just before the picnic, and the savoury smell of pastry and bacon filled the car for the entire journey. When the basket finally was opened and the slices cut, the pie was still warm.

We visited expert bacon and egg pie man Graham King at one of the two Napier bowls clubs where he keeps the greens. I consider myself to be a bowls blueblood – my grandfather was a stalwart of the Edgeware Bowls Club in Christchurch, where I attended afternoon teas and opening day ladies-a-plate lunches. So this was a real pleasure. Bowls and bacon and egg pie.

Jenny's Whisky Roll

In Hastings, Jenny Alcock whipped up her speciality dessert. She's made it on most of the world's continents and it is her standard contribution when she is asked to bring a plate.

2 packets chocolate chip biscuits
5 plain biscuits
100 g butter
1 cup icing sugar
1 egg
½ cup whisky
150 g cooking chocolate chips
butter for chocolate coating

Crush both types of biscuits together in food processor and set aside.

Cream butter and icing sugar together. Add egg and whisky, then add biscuit crumbs.

Grease two pieces of aluminium foil and mould half the mixture into a log shape on each. Wrap the foil around the logs and refrigerate for at least 24 hours.

Before serving melt chocolate in the microwave, adding a good blob of butter. Cover the logs with a generous coating, then put them back into the fridge for a few minutes. Cut into slices 1 cm or more thick.

MAKES 2

JENNY'S WHISKY ROLL IS WONDERFUL
WITH STRAWBERRIES AND STICKY WINE
– OR JUST KEEP IT IN THE FRIDGE AND
HAVE A NIBBLE EVERY TIME YOU OPEN
THE DOOR. THE RECIPE CAN BE MADE
WITH SEVERAL TYPES OF BISCUITS, E.G.,
SUPER WINES, GIRL GUIDE BISCUITS,
DUTCH CINNAMON OR, MY FAVOURITE,
CHOCOLATE CHIP.

RICHARD'S PICNIC MENU

I'm a big fan of a winter picnic, when I get to use my little camping stove to make some thick, hot soup. But this occurs so infrequently they don't really count because 95% of my picnics take place at a beach, by a lake or under the shade of a tree. And they're always best when the day is hot enough to make you want to seek somewhere cool.

Baba Ganoush

This is a really lovely dippy spread thing – and it's my favourite 'secret ingredient' in a casserole of any kind. A tablespoon or two of the rich, garlicky mixture stirred in just before serving always lifts a casserole out of the ordinary and gives me an opportunity to feel smug and self-satisfied. But it's unlikely there would be any left for that if I took it on a picnic . . .

- 2 small to medium-sized eggplants
- 6 cloves garlic, peeled
- 2 Tbsp olive oil for roasting
- salt for eggplant
- juice of 2 lemons
- 1/4 cup tahini
- 1/4 cup plain unsweetened yoghurt
- 1/4 cup extra virgin olive oil
- salt and freshly ground black pepper to taste

Preheat the oven to 180°C.

Cut eggplants in half lengthways and place them in a roasting tin. Poke holes in the flesh and stuff holes with slivers of all but one of the cloves of garlic. Drizzle with olive oil and lightly salt. Roast for 20–30 minutes until the eggplants are soft and lightly browned. Allow to cool.

Put roasted eggplant in a food processor with the remaining clove of raw garlic, lemon juice, tahini, yoghurt and olive oil. Pulse until it reaches a coarse but homogeneous texture. Season with salt and pepper.

MAKES 2 CUPS

Frittata

My number-one picnic standby is in the same realm as bacon and egg pie, but without the pastry, and packed with vegetables. Frittata, Spanish omelette, tortilla, whatever you call it, it's a lot of well-seasoned cooked vegetables bound together in a cheesy egg mixture. This is my favourite version, but go on, express yourself, choose your own preferred vegetables! I added bacon when I cooked the dish on telly because I wanted to make it more like bacon and egg pie, but I really prefer this dish without.

1/4 cup oil
2 red onions, chopped
2 carrots, diced
2 leeks, diced
1 red pepper, diced
2 spring onions, chopped
2/3 cup cooked peas
2 cups diced cooked peeled potato
1/2 cup grated cheddar cheese
1/4 cup crumbled feta
1 Tbsp chopped fresh thyme or other herbs of your choice
6–8 eggs, depending on size
salt and freshly ground black pepper to taste

Preheat the ovenproof dish in the oven at 180°C.

Heat half the oil in a large frypan and cook the onion, carrot, leek and red pepper until softened. Add spring onion, peas, potato, cheeses and herbs. Gently stir in the eggs one by one. Season with salt and pepper.

Carefully tip remaining oil into the very hot ovenproof dish and tilt it so the oil runs over all the inside surfaces. Quickly add the egg, vegetable and cheese mixture and return dish to the oven. Cook at 180°C for 25–40 minutes, depending on the dimensions of your dish. Wide and shallow needs less time, deeper needs more.

You can tell the frittata is cooked when it has puffed up in a dome right to the centre and is firm to the touch.

SERVES 8

Sampler Box Picnic Biscuits

Nowadays the sampler tins are generally sampler boxes and don't come in layers. The biscuit selection has changed a little, but they are still beautiful manufactured items, and there's still the risk you might miss out on a favourite.

1 sampler box biscuits

Open packaging. Eat with manners.

ONE OF THE MEMORABLE FEATURES OF THE FAMILY SUMMER HOLIDAYS OF MY CHILDHOOD WAS THE BISCUIT SAMPLER TIN, TWO LAYERS OF TREATS THAT PROVOKED EXCITEMENT AND ANXIETY IN EQUAL MEASURE. ALL THOSE CHOCOLATE-COATED BISCUITS, THE PINK WAFER BISCUITS, THE SWISS CREAMS — BUT WOULD THE PARENTS, GRANDPARENTS AND SISTER IN THE QUEUE AHEAD OF ME TAKE THE LAST OF THOSE? WOULD I BE LEFT WITH THE PLAIN BISCUITS THAT SOMEONE HAD TO EAT BEFORE THE LOWER LAYER COULD BE REVEALED? SUCH POSSIBILITY FOR PLEASURE LACED WITH SUCH OPPORTUNITY FOR DISAPPOINTMENT.

THE PIE IS A BRILLIANT CONCEPT, A SELF-CONTAINED HOT MEAL. IT DOESN'T DESERVE THE BAD PRESS IT'S BEEN GETTING. THE PIES DON'T MAKE YOU EAT TEN A DAY, OR WASH THEMSELVES DOWN WITH GALLONS OF COKE. ANYWAY, MORE PIES ARE SOLD EACH DAY THAN COPIES OF CUISINE SELL EACH MONTH.

Pies. Just Pies.
Auckland

When I was a university student I spent a great deal of time in the university cafeteria eating pies. The pies in question were of solid construction. People would shove a fork in the middle of the base and nibble around the outside walls and crust, making an ever smaller circle of congealed meat with pastry top and bottom, and did this without so much as a single gravy spillage. I don't remember thinking for a critical instant about the constitution of these pies. They were pies. Pies were pies. We ate them cold, for heaven's sake.

When I was a child we had the occasional bakery pie. As a family, we would split the centre and apply a little Worcestershire sauce into the filling. I found it quite a shock when no one in the uni café looked for the Worcestershire, but instead, without batting an eyelid, drenched the pie and plate in tomato sauce.

My dear mother had a thing for a certain type of mutton pie. These pies, in the variant sold by the Andersons Bay supermarket in the 1970s, had a firm, short crust with straight sides containing a largely empty cavity. What wasn't steam was mutton gristle floating in a liquid that was eight parts mutton fat, one part meat juice and one part salt. I just assumed it was something one needed to grow into liking.

Don's Mince Pie

According to Don, this pie can be served either hot with mashed potatoes and a green vegetable or (my favourite) cold with a freshly tossed salad and garlic bread.

500–600 g beef mince
1 potato, peeled and chopped into 2 cm pieces
1 onion, chopped
1 small carrot, chopped into smallish pieces
a good ½ tsp Marmite
¼ cup water
½ cup frozen peas (not minted)
handful of flour
salt and pepper to taste
1 x 400 g packet frozen short pastry,
   defrosted and allowed to rest

Place mince, potato, onion, carrot and Marmite in a medium-sized pot and add water. Cook over a low-moderate heat, stirring frequently, for 30 minutes. Add peas and cook for another 15–30 minutes.

Sprinkle a smallish handful of flour over mince, stir thoroughly and cook for 5 minutes more. Season with salt and pepper. At end of cooking, allow mince mixture to cool thoroughly.

Preheat the oven to 225°C.

Roll out pastry and use it to line a pie dish. Add the cool filling and finish off with a pastry lid. Place dish on a metal oven tray on a low shelf of the oven. Cook for 15 minutes at 225°C then decrease temperature to 180°C and cook for a further 20 minutes (cooking time may be longer depending on your oven). If you have fan bake, use it in the last 10 minutes to finish off the pie.

SERVES 4

DON LINDEN HAS RECREATED HIS MOTHER'S FAMILY MINCE PIE. IT'S AN ONGOING WORK OF REFINEMENT OF METHOD. HE HAS CONSULTED WIDELY AMONG HIS FAMILY FOR INSIGHTS AND OBSERVATIONS OF HIS MOTHER'S METHOD, AND THE FOLLOWING PIE RECIPE IS A WONDERFUL HOMAGE. AND A DAMN GOOD PIE TOO.

Edita's Apple Pie

Not everyone's idea of a fruit pie is the same. This apple pie from Edita Andrijasevic is an apple pie to her and fellow Serbs, but an apple shortcake to a Kiwi.

2 cups strong or high-grade flour
⅓ cup caster sugar
baking powder on the tip of a knife
4 Tbsp margarine or butter
1 sachet vanilla sugar (or 2 drops vanilla essence)
1 egg yolk
zest of 1 lemon
2 Tbsp sour cream
5 apples
juice of half a lemon
butter and flour to line dish
handful of dry breadcrumbs
50 g sugar mixed with ½ tsp ground cinnamon
icing sugar for dusting

Mix flour, caster sugar and baking powder thoroughly (the best way is to sieve it all into a bowl). Rub margarine in. When mixed well add vanilla sugar, egg yolk, lemon zest and sour cream. Mix until all ingredients are well combined. Cover dough with cling film and allow to chill in fridge for at least an hour.

Peel, core and grate the apples. Pour lemon juice over. Grease a sandwich tin with butter and dust with flour.

Preheat the oven to 180°C.

Roll out half the chilled dough for the base, trim the edges and return what is left of the dough to the fridge. Squeeze the excess moisture from the apple. Evenly sprinkle the breadcrumbs on the pastry base and follow with the apples. Evenly sprinkle the mixture of sugar and cinnamon over the apples. Roll out the remaining dough and cover the pie. Press lightly to set and make some holes in the top using a fork.

Bake for 15–20 minutes or until golden brown. Do the toothpick test to see if it is fully cooked in the middle. Allow pie to cool before dusting with icing sugar.

SERVES 12

Richard's All-Pie Meal

This is a menu is a challenge to the description of what constitutes a pie and also a call to those who give pies bad press – I suggest they might lighten up a bit.

Stuffed Mushrooms

This is an excellent starter to an all-pie meal. Smaller button mushrooms done this way make good finger food and very big flat mushrooms a lovely side dish with steak.

  20 medium-sized flat mushrooms
  4 slices grainy bread
  100 g brie or camembert
  50 g blue cheese
  50 g feta
  50 g ground parmesan (from the cardboard tube)
  2 cloves garlic, peeled and chopped
  1 red onion, chopped
  handful of basil leaves

Preheat the oven to 180°C.

  Separate mushrooms from their stems. Place the stems, bread, cheeses, garlic, red onion and basil leaves in the food processor bowl with the chopping blades. Pulse until the mixture is barely combined. It's best if it retains a very coarse texture, with discernible pieces of bread, onion, and various cheeses visible.

  Divide this stuffing between the mushroom caps, pressing it onto the cap, covering all the gills. Bake on an oven tray for 10–15 minutes. Grill to lightly brown the tops.

SERVES 8

I MIGHT BE ACCUSED OF BEING A BIT SOFT IN MY DEFINITION OF 'PIE'. BUT I SAY STUFFED MUSHROOMS CAN BE A PIE IF YOU CONSIDER THE MUSHROOM AS THE PASTRY AND THE BREADY CHEESY TOPPING AS A FILLING. IT'S AN OPEN-FACED, MUSHROOM-CRUSTED PIE.

Dressed Pie

This is my pie of pies. The potato-top pie gone flash.

2 onions, finely chopped
2 carrots, grated
oil for frying
500 g beef mince
salt and pepper for mince filling
2 Tbsp cornflour
4 Tbsp water
6 potatoes, peeled
¼ cup milk
2 Tbsp butter
salt and white pepper for
  potato topping
1 egg, beaten
pastry (use Graham's recipe on page 26,
  or buy shortcrust pastry from the supermarket)
2 cups frozen peas, boiled in salted water for 30 minutes and drained
1 x 410 g can beetroot

In a frypan brown onion and carrot in oil. Add mince and allow to brown. Season carefully with salt and pepper. Mix cornflour with water and beat this slurry into the mince. Use more if the mince is particularly runny. Allow to cool.

Boil the potatoes and, while they are still hot, mash in milk, butter, salt and pepper. When almost cool add the beaten egg and combine well.

Preheat the oven to 170°C. Line well-greased individual pie tins with rolled-out pastry. Fill pastry shells with cold mince. Cover tops with mashed potato. Bake for 45 minutes.

Remove pies from oven. Break crusts with spoon and force mushy peas into the potato. Force a slice of beetroot into the potato beside the peas.

Look at what you are doing and make it beautiful. Yes, that's right, beautiful!

Allow to stand until the pies have cooled sufficiently to be eaten without removing the skin from inside your guests' mouths. Serve with a ladleful of packet gravy over the top if you are so inclined. I am inclined that way myself.

MAKES 8–10 PIES

Richard's World Famous (because he says so) Cheesecake

The dessert pie for this menu is a cheesecake. A baked cheesecake I made a thousand times years ago when I was in the restaurant business. It was so popular it almost single-handedly paid the rent.

1 packet digestive biscuits
⅓ packet gingernuts
2 Tbsp flour
100 g butter, melted
4 eggs, separated
zest and juice of 1 lemon
¾ cup sugar
375 g cream cheese
2 Tbsp sour cream
2 Tbsp sambuca

Preheat the oven to 160°C.

Use a food processor to break the biscuits into crumbs. Transfer crumbs to a bowl, add flour and melted butter and combine. Tip this mixture into an 18–20 cm springform tin and press with your fingers to form base and sides.

Place egg yolks, lemon zest and juice, sugar, cream cheese and sour cream in the food processor. Whizz until smooth then add sambuca and whizz some more.

In a separate bowl beat the egg whites until they form peaks. Fold the egg yolk mixture into the whites and tip into the biscuit crust.

Bake for 50 minutes, until puffed up and rounded.

SERVES 12

THE BOIL-UP RUNS CONTRARY TO ALL MY DEFAULT SETTINGS ABOUT HOW TO COOK MEAT IN THAT THERE IS NO BROWNING, ONLY BOILING. HOWEVER, I'M DRAWN TO THE WAY IT IS MADE TO SERVE A CROWD, AND I REALLY LIKE THE WAY THAT, WITH CARE, YOU GET WELL-COOKED CHUNKS OF MEAT AND VEGETABLE ALONG WITH A FANTASTIC BROTH. I'M DEFINITELY A CONVERT TO THE METHOD.

Some Unfamiliar Things
Far North

Regional food is not the preserve of the French and the Italians. It's a feature of New Zealand cooking too. All of the dishes prepared in this chapter by our guest cooks were unfamiliar to me, Maori specialities made in hundreds of Kiwi kitchens but never in mine. But it's as much about the gap between City New Zealand and Rural New Zealand as it is about the different culinary traditions of pakeha and Maori.

In my neck of the South Island woods, any shellfish other than oyster was bait. Bait to catch actual fish. Fish with fins and eyes. I had heard about other shellfish that were considered delicacies, toheroa and tuatua amongst them, but I didn't have much to do with them except as illustrations in a book of New Zealand shells. In the far north, however, the tuatua is part of the local way of life that makes it into many a fritter.

The boil-up runs contrary to all my default settings about how to cook meat in that there is no browning, only boiling. It's wet hangi and perfect for a crowd. Complete in its containment of the essences of each ingredient, it is an almost exact match of the French dish pot-au-feu, or the Italian bolito misto. And burnt sugar boiled pudding is not for the faint-hearted. It's a very tricky process to make it, and burning the sugar creates a strong odour that clings to the drapes.

My menu is for a pretty hard-out dinner party. There's a bit of work, and a fair amount of advance preparation, but that is often the best thing for a cook who wishes to be an attentive member of the company at the table.

Ray's Kumara and Tuatua Fritters

100 tuatua
1 Tbsp crushed garlic
1 cup flour
1½ tsp baking powder
½ tsp ground coriander
¼ tsp ground cumin
salt and pepper to taste
½ cup milk
2 eggs
1 cup grated kumara, softened
   in frypan with oil
2 Tbsp chopped parsley
¾ cup olive oil
dipping sauce (see recipe opposite)

DIPPING SAUCE

1 Tbsp cider vinegar
3 Tbsp brown sugar
1 tsp finely chopped fresh chilli
   or chilli sauce
1 Tbsp fresh chives, chopped
½ tsp soy sauce

Combine ingredients well and heat.

Put tuatua in seawater and leave overnight, then steam them until they open. Discard the unopened ones.

Chop steamed tuatua in a food processor, adding the garlic.

Sift flour, baking powder, spices and seasoning into a bowl. Make a well in dry ingredients and then add milk and eggs. Stir until combined. Add tuatua, softened kumara and parsley.

Heat oil in a frypan and lower heaped tablespoons of the mixture into the pan, making sure each spoonful is separated from the others. You can slightly squash the spoonfuls down. Fry until fritters look cooked, turning after 2 minutes. Remove them from pan and allow to drain on a paper towel.

SERVE WITH DIPPING SAUCE.

RAY WOOLF, ENTERTAINMENT LEGEND, IS A MAN OF THE FAR NORTH.
IN A HOUSE MADE BY THE SWEAT OF HIS (AND HIS WIFE'S) BROW.
HE KNOCKED UP SOME FRITTERS WITH TUATUA HE HAD COLLECTED
FROM THE BEACH YOU CAN SEE FROM HIS VERANDA.

CHARLES DUNN, AN UNDEFEATED HEAVYWEIGHT BOXING CHAMPION OF NEW ZEALAND, MADE A VERY THOUGHTFULLY EXECUTED BOIL-UP FOR ME. THE DISH COOKED OVER MANY HOURS, BUT EACH ADDITION OF NEW INGREDIENTS WAS MADE AT A MOMENT SELECTED WITH THE CERTAINTY OF EXPERIENCE AND THE CONFIDENCE OF A MAN IN TUNE WITH HIS INGREDIENTS. IT WAS A GREAT PLEASURE TO SEE IT MADE AND AN EVEN GREATER PLEASURE TO EAT IT.

Charles's Boil-Up

A boil-up must be served with good Maori bread, and is best followed by peach jam and fried bread. Traditionally the second cooking is the tastiest, so if there are leftovers just reboil and enjoy.

beef brisket
mutton neck chops
salt and pepper to taste
potatoes
kumara, cut into large chunks
pumpkin, cut into large chunks
kamokamo, cut into large chunks
cabbage, roughly cut up
wild spinach

Other meats you could use include:

pig's head
pork bones
bacon bones
trotters
hocks
almost any other
    bones of lamb or beef

Place meat in a large pot, cover with water and boil until soft. It usually takes 2–3 hours. Add salt and pepper. Three-quarters of an hour before serving, add potato, kumara, pumpkin and kamokamo to the cooking pot. Add the rest of the veges 15 minutes before serving.

NOTE: When it comes to a boil-up, the ingredients are determined by availability – seasonal and otherwise. Kumara, potatoes, pumpkin and kamokamo are musts. When watercress and puha are in season these would be the best vegetables to use, in place of the cabbage and wild spinach, but they take a good hour to cook.

Gloria's Burnt Sugar Pudding

This recipe is a gamble. But if by a stroke of luck you were to correctly burn the sugar, and then by some miracle of fate add just the right amount to the mixture, you would be very pleased you made the attempt. But be warned, burning the sugar makes a very strong smell. Gloria's husband prefers she make it only in the marae kitchen.

2 cups sugar
boiling water
3 cups flour
125 g butter
1 tsp cinnamon
1 tsp baking powder
1 tsp baking soda
1 tsp rum essence
1 egg

Put half the sugar into a pot. Melt the sugar and as it starts to burn add some boiling water. Mix and leave it to cool.

Put the rest of the sugar into a bowl with the flour and add butter. Rub butter into flour and sugar. Add cinnamon and baking powder.

Dissolve baking soda in ½ cup burnt sugar water and then add this to the butter/flour/sugar mixture. Add rum essence and egg.

Intuitively judge how much more of the burnt sugar water to add to the dry ingredients as you start mixing it. Combine well.

Place mixture in a pre-wetted and wrung-out calico bag. Tie up the bag firmly, making sure you leave a little room at the top for the pudding to expand as it cooks.

Put the bag in a pot of boiling water and boil for about 2 hours.

SERVES 8–10

MAKING BURNT SUGAR IS NOT STRAIGHTFORWARD. I WATCHED GLORIA WIJOHN COOK THE SUGAR, I WATCHED THE SUGAR BROWN IN THE PAN, COOK IN THE PAN AND THEN BURN IN THE PAN. I WATCHED AS GLORIA WATCHED AND BURNT THE SUGAR, AND BURNT IT SOME MORE. THEN, AT A POINT GOVERNED BY EXPERIENCE AND INTUITION, GLORIA POURED IN BOILING WATER. AND THERE IT WAS – BURNT SUGAR. HOW SHE CHOSE THE MOMENT CANNOT BE EXPLAINED.

THE 'IMPRESS WITH EASE' DINNER PARTY

The more I look at this menu the hungrier I get.

Best Mussel Fritters

I made this recipe up from scratch. Not a common event. And the result is so good I'll never try to make anything up again. The key to this great success is getting the mussel meat out of the shells uncooked. There is no need to get the mussel out in one piece, you're going to chop them up, so just hack them out any old how.

2 cups chopped raw mussels
1 carrot, finely grated
2 fresh red chillies,
   finely chopped
handful of fresh coriander,
   roughly chopped
1 clove garlic, peeled and
   finely minced
5 slices white toast bread,
   cut into 5 mm cubes
2 eggs
⅓ cup flour
salt and pepper to taste
½ cup peanut oil for frying

Combine ingredients (except oil). Heat peanut oil in a frypan and shallow fry spoonfuls of the mixture. Allow to drain on paper towels.

Serve lightly salted with lemon, lime or sweet chilli sauce, or some other dipping sauce, or nothing else at all.

MAKES 16

NOT MANY CITY DWELLERS HAVE TUATUA GROWING AT THE END OF THEIR ROAD. BUT ONE THING IS FOR SURE, THE LOCAL SUPERMARKET, OR THE ONE NEXT SUBURB OVER, WILL HAVE A TUB OF GREEN-LIPPED MUSSELS.

Best Roast Duck with a Boil-Up Method

This is the tenderest, moistest roast duck imaginable, with the best sauce ever. It's everything about roast duck that is good, at the same time as being a bit like honey soy chicken nibbles – and find me someone who doesn't like those. The boil-first method removes any possibility of toughness or dryness in the bird, and having the lion's share of the preparation completed the day before makes for a more relaxed cook at the party.

1 onion, cut into chunks
1 stalk celery, cut into chunks
1 duck
small nub of ginger root, sliced
½ cup port
½ cup light soy sauce
juice of 6 oranges
½ cup brown sugar
salt and pepper to taste

Start cooking the day before you wish to serve the roast duck.

Put onion and celery inside the duck. Place duck in a large pot and add cold water until the duck is almost, but not quite, covered. Bring to the boil and then reduce to a simmer and put the lid on the pot. Allow to simmer for 1 hour.

Turn the duck over in the water and add the ginger, port, soy sauce, orange juice and brown sugar. Cover and simmer for another hour, then allow to cool in pot.

Carefully remove duck from pot to plate, cover and refrigerate overnight. Strain the liquid into a jug or bowl and also refrigerate.

The following day, preheat the oven to 200°C. Remove fat from reserved liquid, and heat liquid in saucepan to reduce to about 1 cup.

Cut duck in half, lengthways along backbone. Carefully remove ribcage and backbone. Place duck in an ovenproof serving dish, skin side up, and cook in oven for 30–40 minutes.

Add seasoning to taste to the reduced liquid, which is now the sauce.

SERVES 4

Somewhat inexplicably, in my mind the classic crisp-skinned *Duck a L'Orange* garnish is a handful of sparklers, lit as you bring the dish to the table. Sparklers and a robust hazard management programme.

Best Crème Brûlée

This is another dish where the preparation comes the day before, leaving very little to be done on the day. My recipe uses a large dish. It's also nice to make it in individual portions (I use coffee cups), but the cooking time must be considerably reduced. Check the Brûlées are cooked by gently shaking one. If it is uncooked, the centre will wobble mightily, if cooked it will wobble slightly.

    3 cups cream
    8 egg yolks
    1 cup sugar
    1½ tsp vanilla essence
    pinch of salt
    6 Tbsp caster sugar for topping

Preheat the oven to 130°C.
  Place all the ingredients (except caster sugar) in a large bowl. Whisk to combine. Pour into an ovenproof dish and put this dish into a roasting tin. Add hot water to the roasting tin until it comes halfway up the sides of the brûlée dish.
  Bake for 1½ hours or until set. Remove from oven, allow to cool and refrigerate overnight.
  Just before serving, remove baked custard from the fridge and set about brûlée-ing it as follows.
  Cover the top with a thin layer of caster sugar. Using a brûlée torch from the kitchenware shop, or a similar gas torch from the garage, work the flame slowly over the sugar until it begins to liquidise and caramelise. It's a knack. You can only get better at it with practice.

SERVES 6

THE BEST DESSERT IN THE
WORLD IS CRÈME BRÛLÉE.
THIS HAS BEEN PROVEN BY
GENERATIONS OF RIGHT-
THINKING PEOPLE. IT'S SIMPLE,
HAS THE MOST WONDERFUL
RANGE OF TEXTURES AND IS
EASY TO MAKE. RESTAURANTS
NEVER SEEM TO BE ABLE TO
LEAVE IT ALONE, ALWAYS
ADDING THINGS LIKE BERRIES,
RHUBARB AND NUTS. DON'T
RUIN A PERFECTLY GOOD
DISH BY DISPLAYING YOUR
INVENTIVENESS — MAKE A
PERFECT, SIMPLE UN-MESSED-
WITH CRÈME BRÛLÉE.

THE BLUFF OYSTER IS EMBLEMATIC OF FISHERIES MANAGEMENT IN NEW ZEALAND. IF THE BLUFF OYSTER FISHERY IS REPORTED TO BE IN GOOD SHAPE MOST PEOPLE FEEL THAT ALL IS WELL IN FISH STOCKS ACROSS THE BOARD. BUT OYSTERS ARE ALWAYS GOING TO BE UNDER PRESSURE. THERE SEEM TO BE FAR MORE PEOPLE WANTING TO EAT THE OYSTERS THAN THERE ARE OYSTERS.

Sunday Tea
Southland

There are more reasons to go to Southland than I can recount. But were I to try, high on that list I'd put: the great beaches with a warm ocean current making swimming warmer cleaner and generally better in all ways than further up the east coast; the people, content and welcoming; Bluff oysters; and the climate, changeable, rainy weather that's perfect for puddings.

It's a perfect place to make a Sunday tea menu, for it illustrates the appropriate state of mind better than anywhere else. The ideal Sunday tea is set against a backdrop of a warm and homely room, curtains pulled, coal cracking and splitting on the fire while the rain hammers on a tin roof. This is the place for dishes that are big, warm and round-flavoured.

Our first stop was at Bluff to pay homage to the oyster. Who am I kidding, it was a charade designed to let me eat as many Bluff oysters as possible and get paid to do it. Then it was time for the other Southland speciality, the swede. For pudding we were lucky to go to Southland Boys' High and have their champion cook prepare a jam pudding for us.

Spencer's Battered Oysters

2 eggs
½ cup flour
2 dozen oysters
flour for dusting
oil for frying

To make the batter, place eggs, flour and your preferred amount of juice from the oysters (instead of adding salt) in a bowl. Mix with an egg beater.

Cover the oysters in flour and dunk them in the batter to cover thoroughly. Shallow fry in hor oil until golden in a hot pan.

SERVES 4

Spencer Morrison is 'Mr Oyster' come oyster festival time. He has been known to recite poems about the oyster while wearing a kilt. He's a heck of a fella, a wood carver, a grandfather and keenly involved in the local community. He went against his principles to cook oysters for us. Spencer quite rightly sees no point in cooking them when they are perfectly delicious raw but I argued that *Kiwi Kitchen* is a cooking show and he obliged.

SWEDE SEEMS TO
HAVE A HOLD OVER
THE MINDS OF PEOPLE
FROM SOUTHLAND.
MANY OF THEM TAKE
IT QUITE PERSONALLY
IF YOU EXPRESS
YOUR DISLIKE OF
THIS VEGETABLE
WITHIN THE RANGE
OF THEIR HEARING.
BELIEVE ME, I KNOW
THIS BECAUSE I'VE
RECEIVED A LOT OF
CROSS LETTERS!

Patricia's Mashed Swede

If you've never tried swede, here's the way some swede eaters eat their swede, and if you have tried swede, why are you reading how to boil it? You either know what to do, or you're going to be cooking something else.

1 swede
1 tsp salt
dash of cream
freshly ground black pepper to taste

Peel swede and cut into cubes. Cover with water in a pot, add salt and bring to the boil. Simmer until tender. Drain. Mash with the cream and a good grind of black pepper.

SERVES 4

IN PICTURESQUE ATHOL, PATRICIA SOPER COOKED SWEDE AND TERRIFIED ME WITH STORIES OF SWEDE FAIRS WHERE PEOPLE CREATED RECIPES FOR SWEDE PAVLOVA. ENOUGH TO GIVE A PERSON NIGHTMARES. I TRIED SWEDE COOKED AND I TRIED SWEDE RAW, AND IF I WERE TO EAT IT AGAIN I WOULD CHOOSE RAW. IT WAS REALLY RATHER DELICIOUS, CRISP AND WITH A HINT OF THE BRASSICA FLAVOUR.

Ethan's Jam Pudding with Sauce Anglaise and Berry Coulis

raspberry jam
60 g butter
60 g sugar
1 egg
120 g self-raising flour
1 Tbsp milk
sauce anglaise (see recipe opposite)
berry coulis (see recipe opposite)
whipped cream to serve

Preheat the oven to 180°C.

Grease six individual ovenproof moulds. Place a small quantity of jam in the bottom of each mould.

Cream butter and sugar, then add egg and beat together. Fold in self-raising flour and then mix in milk.

Spoon batter into moulds to come just up to half way, then add some more jam and top with more batter. Place moulds in a roasting tin with boiling water that comes half way up the sides of the moulds. Cover with aluminium foil and bake for 40 minutes.

Keep warm until ready to serve.

To serve, turn the jam pudding onto a plate. Spoon some of the anglaise onto the plate then place drops of coulis in the anglaise and pull through with a skewer. Serve with a quenelle of whipped cream.

MAKES 6

It's wonderful to see that Southland Boys' High offers cooking training. Student Ethan Flack has gone on to represent New Zealand in culinary eventing and is heading towards a career in the kitchen. He makes a pretty flash steamed jam pudding that, by his own account, makes him a total babe magnet.

Sauce Anglaise

250 ml milk
2 egg yolks
25 g caster sugar
2-3 drops vanilla essence

Place milk in a saucepan and bring to the boil. Meanwhile mix yolks, sugar and vanilla in a bowl until they are light and creamy. Pour in boiled milk and mix until smooth.

Place bowl over a pot of boiling water and cook until custard thickens and coats the back of the spoon.

Allow to cool slightly.

Berry Coulis

1 regular punnet raspberries
1/4 cup sugar
1/4 cup water

Place ingredients in a saucepan and heat. Whizz in a food processor then pass through a sieve.

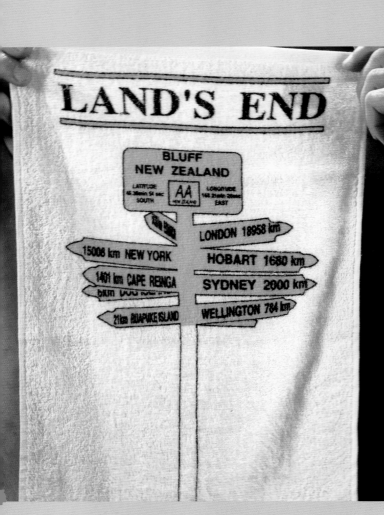

RICHARD'S SUNDAY TEA

Perfect for a cheering up a cold and rainy Sunday night.

Grand Central Station Oyster Stew

The secret is cooking, or possibly not cooking, the oysters just right. They need to be warmed in the sauce, but hardly cooked. If they were eggs they would be coddled. Serve with a few bits of well-dried toast.

    1 dozen oysters
    6 Tbsp cream
    ½–1 tsp celery salt
    dash of Worcestershire sauce
    freshly ground black pepper to taste
    toasts for serving

Drain the oysters, reserving the oyster juice.
   Heat a heavy pan on a medium-high heat. Add cream and drained oysters and a couple of tablespoons of oyster juice. Add celery salt and Worcestershire sauce.
   Cook, shaking the pan, until the oysters start to firm up. This will be about 30 seconds after the cream gets to boiling.
   Remove oysters to serving dishes. Reduce cream mixture until slightly thickened and syrupy. Grind pepper into the sauce and tip it over the oysters.
   Serve with toasts.

SERVES 2–4

MY NUMBER-ONE FOOD HERO, JULIA CHILD, PEERED OVER THE COUNTER OF THE OYSTER BAR AT NEW YORK'S GRAND CENTRAL STATION, MADE NOTE OF WHAT WENT INTO THE RESTAURANT'S FAMOUS OYSTER STEW AND SUBSEQUENTLY PUBLISHED THE RECIPE. WHEN I WAS IN THE RESTAURANT BUSINESS I MADE THIS DISH ON AND OFF FOR MANY YEARS.

Sausage Casserole

6 plain sausages
6 apples, peeled and sliced
4 onions, peeled and sliced
30 g butter
salt
2 dessertspoons flour
1 Tbsp mustard powder
4 Tbsp brown sugar
3 Tbsp cider vinegar

Put sausages in a saucepan and just cover with water. Bring to the boil, then simmer for 5 minutes. Leave them in their water to cool.

Place sliced apple and onion in a heavy-bottomed saucepan with butter, a little salt and 1 cup of the water in which the sausages were poached (we shall grandly call this 'the poaching liquid'). Bring to the boil, give a good stir, cover, turn down the heat and simmer for 30 minutes.

Preheat the oven to 180°C.

Peel the sausages, disposing of the skin. Slice the sausage meat into thickish chunks.

Mix together flour, mustard and sugar. Toss sausage chunks in this mixture. Combine this with the apple and onion mixture, add vinegar and mix well.

Tip all this into a casserole dish and add poaching liquid until there is just enough liquid in the casserole to almost cover the sliced sausages.

Bake, covered, for 45 minutes to 1 hour.

SERVES 4–6

My mother made sausage casseroles often, though not as often as I would have liked. It came in many versions with different ingredients – tomato paste, curry powder and the like – that provided variety in a world where there were only sausages or chipolatas. There were no venison, pineapple and cumin sausages or Polish sausages, just recipes to alter plain old sausages and make them seem interesting.

Jam Tart

1 cup flour
75 g butter, cut up
3 Tbsp sugar
1 egg yolk
couple of drops of lemon juice
cold water for pastry
1 cup jam

Preheat the oven to 160°C.

Rub flour and butter together with your fingers in a bowl. Keep going for 5-10 minutes, until it achieves a crumbly consistency like sand.

Add sugar, egg yolk, lemon juice and a few tablespoons of cold water. Combine. Add a little more water if needed until the mixture just clings together in a firm dough.

Roll out two-thirds of the pastry dough on a floured surface and use it to line a pie dish. Trim off excess pastry. Fill the tart with a layer of jam. Roll out remaining pastry dough and cut into strips to decorate the top of the pie with pastry lattice. Bake for 20 minutes.

SERVES 6

THE JAM TART WAS A REGULAR PART OF THE PUDDING SCHEDULE WHEN I WAS GROWING UP. IT'S NOT ABOUT SO MUCH THESE DAYS, AS PEOPLE REALLY DON'T MAKE JAM. THERE'S NO NEED TO FIND A WAY TO USE UP LAST SEASON'S JAM WHILE PUTTING THE EXPECTED DAILY PUDDING ON THE FAMILY TABLE. I USUALLY USE SUPERMARKET PASTRY WHEN I'M COOKING A PIE AT HOME, BUT THIS DISH IS NOTHING IF YOU BUY THE PASTRY READY-MADE. THIS ROUGH SHORTCRUST IS NOT A COMPLEX PREPARATION, SO HERE'S A CHANCE FOR ANYONE WHO THINKS MAKING PASTRY IS HARD TO ROLL UP THEIR SLEEVES AND DISCOVER THAT IT'S NOT DIFFICULT AT ALL.

NEW TRENDS COME ALONG ALL THE TIME. THEY LOOK DIFFERENT WHEN YOU LOOK BACK AT THEM. NOUVELLE CUISINE AND FONDUE WERE DEFINITELY TRENDS, BUT IT'S NOT FAIR TO CALL VEGETARIANISM A TREND. I FIRST ENCOUNTERED THE IDEA OF CHOOSING NOT TO EAT MEAT AS A CHILD. IT SEEMED ODD AND SLIGHTLY UNPATRIOTIC WHAT WITH ALL THOSE SHEEP.

Time Travel
Wellington

For this episode we went back in time to the 1980s, the decade I stumbled into the restaurant business. I had helped mum in the home kitchen and had worked in an institution kitchen under the direction of an ex-army chef. I found myself waiting tables, then made the switch to the kitchen in a Wellington restaurant.

It was a great time to be restauranting. The restaurants offered much better experiences than today's – and also much worse, sometimes in the same restaurant. Peter Gordon was at the Sugar Club, Lois Daish was at the Mt Cook Café and a couple of fellas were doing a fine job of multi-course nouvelle cuisine for a lot of money at Petit Lyon. One of those fellas was Martin Bosley, who decades later passed on his snails recipe to Kiwi Kitchen viewers.

People were definitely getting more adventurous with food. Mexican, Middle Eastern and Indian restaurants joined the Chinese takeaways in the fight for the 'ethnic' food dollar. Even the steak houses started providing a Vegetarian Option, which from 1984 until 1987 was fettuccini with pesto. Everywhere, without exception.

In the 1980s, no one, diner or restaurateur, really knew what they were doing. It was probably a good thing.

Martin's Snails in Bloody Mary Jelly

This dish is a great example of the experimentation that was going on in restaurants in the 1980s. Until the day he came on *Kiwi Kitchen*, restaurateur Martin Bosley had never tried these snails for himself. At the price he was charging for this dish back in the eighties, he'd have been a fool to waste it on himself. Try it if you are adventurous – but bear in mind that Martin himself described it as 'absolutely disgusting'.

2 gelatine leaves
3/4 cup tomato juice
2 Tbsp vodka
splash of Worcestershire sauce
splash of Tabasco sauce
1 tsp horseradish sauce
pinch of celery salt
freshly ground black pepper to taste
12 canned snails, washed thoroughly under cold running water
baby lettuce leaves
small bunches of fresh herbs

Soak gelatine leaves in cold water until soft. Drain water and squeeze excess from softened leaves. Place them in a saucepan with the tomato juice and heat through gently to dissolve.

Pour hot tomato juice mixture over vodka. Stir in the Worcestershire, Tabasco and horseradish sauces, celery salt and pepper. Place three snails in each of four round moulds (we used a muffin tray). Pour the Bloody Mary around the snails and refrigerate until set.

Turn out the jelly and garnish with the lettuce leaves and herb sprigs.

SERVES 4

NOUVELLE CUISINE MARKS THE BEGINNING OF THE DAYS OF THE CHEF AS A CELEBRITY. IT'S SUCH 'LOOK AT ME' FOOD. IT'S AS IF THE CHEFS ARE SAYING THAT NATURE AND CREATION NEEDS A BIT OF A HAND FROM THEM TO MAKE A MEAL WORTHY OF FALLING UNDER THE GAZE OF THE REFINED HUMAN. WHATEVER IT WAS — OR IS — YOU CAN STILL HAVE A BIT OF FUN RESURRECTING THE STYLE AT HOME. MARTIN BOSLEY IS ONE OF THE MOST HIGHLY ESTEEMED RESTAURATEURS OF THE COUNTY TODAY, AND HE WAS A TOP PRACTITIONER OF THE ART OF NOUVELLE CUISINE BACK IN THE GOOD OLD DAYS OF THE EIGHTIES.

In the 1980s vegetarianism became more than a moral commitment, it was a slightly cool lifestyle choice. Nicky Owers, president of the Wellington branch of the New Zealand Vegetarian Society, dug out the cookbook she used in the 1980s and made Nepalese Vegetable Curry for us.

Nicky's Nepalese Vegetable Curry

Any other vegetables may be substituted instead of those in the recipe. If you like it hot, or if you've been to India, add another chilli or two.

4 Tbsp ghee or butter
2 onions, chopped
1 bay leaf, broken up
2 green peppers, chopped
1 fresh red chilli
6 cloves garlic, peeled
5 cm piece root ginger, chopped
2 tsp salt
1/2 tsp black pepper
1/2 tsp ground turmeric
2 Tbsp ground coriander
1 Tbsp ground cumin
1 kg potatoes, peeled and cubed
1 cauliflower, cut in florets
6 spring onions, chopped
2 cups peas
6 tomatoes, quartered
1 cup hot water

Heat ghee or butter in a large deep frypan and cook onion until golden. Add bay leaf, green pepper, chilli, garlic, ginger, salt, pepper, and spices. Stir in potatoes and fry until browned. Add remaining ingredients. Cook gently until vegetables are tender.

SERVES 6

Holly's Chocolate Fondue

This is purportedly the original recipe for chocolate fondue created in the 1950s at New York's Chalet Suisse Restaurant (no longer in business) by chef Konrad Egli.

3 x 100 g Toblerone bars, broken into pieces
½ cup cream
2 Tbsp kirsch, brandy or Cointreau
orange or tangerine segments
sliced strawberries or bananas
angelfood cake or ladyfingers, cut in chunks
profiteroles or puff pastry fingers

Combine the first three ingredients in a saucepan or fondue dish. Stir over low heat until the chocolate is melted smooth. Dunk the fruit, cake and pastry in the melted chocolate.

SERVES 6–8

FONDUE WAS STILL KNOCKING AROUND SUBURBAN NEW ZEALAND IN THE 1980s. IT'S A DISH THAT GETS MADE ONLY BECAUSE YOU HAVE A SET IN THE CUPBOARD. HOLLY FULLER OWNS FIVE FONDUE SETS. IF I UNDERSTAND HER CORRECTLY, TO THIS DAY SHE KNOCKS OUT FONDUE PARTIES ON A REGULAR BASIS.

Richard's Eighties Menu

Which by happy coincidence is also all vegetarian.

Chilli con Queso

This chilli and cheese dip is very quick and easy to make. The amount of dairy will keep smiles on the faces of dairy farmers. Serve it warm.

2 small onions, chopped
1 clove garlic, peeled and
   finely chopped
1 spring onion, chopped
juice of 1 lime
$1/4$ cup water
6 Tbsp sour cream
250 g cream cheese
10 pickled jalapeno slices
   (depending how much
   you like jalapeno)
2 cups grated cheese
corn chips to serve

Put onion, garlic, spring onion, lime juice and water in a small saucepan and bring to the boil. Turn down the heat, cover and cook slowly for 5 minutes.
  Add remaining ingredients (except corn chips) and remove from heat. Whizz with stick blender or in a food processor until roughly combined.
  Serve immediately with corn chips.

SERVES 6-8

MEXICAN FOOD WAS ONE OF THE GREAT REVELATIONS OF THE 1980S. I WAS A REGULAR AT THE MEXICAN CANTINA, WHICH SERVED THE BEST MEXICAN FOOD I'VE HAD IN NEW ZEALAND. IT OPERATED OUT OF PREMISES WITH BOOTHS THAT LOOKED LIKE SHEEP PENS, APPROPRIATE GIVEN THE QUEUE OF DINERS WAITING FOR A TABLE. IT SPAWNED A CORN CHIP FACTORY THAT, YEARS AFTER ITS MASTERMIND, JENNY BURNS, HAS PASSED ON TO ETERNAL REST, FILLS SUPERMARKET SHELVES WITH THE MEXICANA BRAND OF CORN CHIP. THEIR UNFLAVOURED CHIP IS FAR AND AWAY THE BEST AVAILABLE IN SUPERMARKETS.

Roast Spiced Vegetables

This vegetable curry is a winner – everyone I've ever met loves roast vegetable cubes, even more so if they are coated in a spiced crust and given a curry sauce. I make this dish often.

 ⅓ cup flour
 2 Tbsp curry powder
 3 tsp salt
 3 potatoes, peeled and cubed
 1 kumara, peeled and cubed
 1 large onion, diced
 ¼ pumpkin, peeled and cubed
 3 Tbsp oil
 ½ cauliflower, cut in small florets
 1 eggplant, cubed
 1 zucchini, cubed
 1 red pepper, cubed
 ¼ cup chopped fresh coriander
 rice to serve
 curry sauce to serve (see recipe opposite)

Preheat the oven to 200°C.
  In a supermarket bag put half the flour, half the curry powder and half the salt. Add the potato, kumara, onion and pumpkin and shake to coat the vegetables with flour, spice and salt. Tip this into a roasting tin with the oil. Cook in the oven for 30 minutes, shaking the tin every so often.
  Put the rest of the flour, curry powder and salt in the supermarket bag, add the remaining vegetables, shake and add to the roasting tin.
  Cook for a further 20–30 minutes, shaking or gently turning with a fish slice every so often.
  Toss with fresh coriander and serve with rice and curry sauce.

SERVES 6

Curry Sauce

1 Tbsp oil
1 tsp cumin seeds
3 cloves garlic, peeled and
  finely chopped
1 fresh red chilli, finely chopped
5 cm ginger root, finely chopped
1 onion, finely chopped
handful of curry leaves (optional)
1 tsp salt
1 x 400 ml can coconut cream

Heat oil in a small saucepan. Add
cumin seeds and cook for 20 seconds,
then add garlic, chilli and ginger. Fry
for a minute, shaking and stirring.
Add onion, stir together and then add
the curry leaves and salt. Cook, stirring
occasionally, for 2 minutes.
  Add coconut cream, bring to the boil
then remove from heat. Reheat when
needed.

Liquorice Ice-Cream

This is one of the few home-made, no-churn ice-cream recipes that remains soft enough to scoop when you retrieve it from the freezer. It's a wacky pale mucky green colour and is one of those things that folk will either love or hate.

250 g liquorice
boiling water
500 ml cream, whipped
3 egg whites
½ cup sugar

Break up liquorice and place in a bowl. Barely cover liquorice with boiling water. Allow to soak for 30 minutes.

Purée liquorice and its water in a blender. Fold whipped cream and liquorice together.

Beat egg whites slowly, adding sugar, until peaks form. Gently fold beaten white into the cream and liquorice mixture.

Put in freezer.

SERVES 8

IN THE 1980s THERE WAS A RESTAURANT IN WELLINGTON CALLED JAVA. IT WAS FAMOUS FOR ITS LIQUORICE ICE-CREAM – AND EVEN MORE FAMOUS FOR BEING A RESTAURANT WITH A KITCHEN FULL OF WOMEN.

MEATBALLS, RISSOLES, MEATLOAF, CHILLI CON CARNE, SPAGHETTI BOLOGNAISE AND LASAGNE ARE JUST PART OF THE CANON OF MINCE DISHES THAT GRACE OUR TABLES. MY MOTHER'S MINCE WHICH STARTED OUT AS MINCE ON TOAST HAD AN ONGOING LIFE: AS SPAGHETTI SAUCE AND THEN, WITH THE ADDITION OF CURRY POWDER AND A FEW SULTANAS, IT BECAME CURRY.

Mince, Glorious Mince
Central Otago

This chapter is a fusion of two things I love dearly. Central Otago and all mince dishes. And although mince was the excuse for going to Central, you will get off lightly — there is actually only one mince dish from our Kiwis in their Kitchens. The other two dishes are the very best in plain fare, and have done their part in raising family loads of children to head into the world in robust health, only to fritter away all that good health on takeaways and processed food. But that's another story.

The first of these wonderful, health-giving, unassuming dishes is one of my mother's standards. You could do far worse than to knock out a batch of Scotch Broth to ward off winter ailments. It's the perfect restorative gift for a friend or neighbour recovering from illness, or a sustaining gift to a family with a new child in the house. The gift of meaty broth never goes out of fashion.

The second dish is a Nicaraguan take on the New Zealand stand-by, mince on toast. This was a frank meeting of mince cultures which was handled with dignity and aplomb by both nations. And the third dish harks back to a time when Kiwis ate pudding, not dessert, they ate it every night, and they never got fat.

Ian and Susie's Scotch Broth

FOR THE STOCK:
2 onions, roughly chopped
1 venison shank (or 5 slices beef shin)
oil for frying
salt and pepper to taste
2 parsnips, cut into chunks
1 small leek, roughly chopped
1 celery stalk, cut into chunks
4 cloves garlic, peeled and chopped

TO MAKE THE SOUP:
2 carrots, grated
1 parsnip, diced
1 onion, finely chopped
2 small leeks, roughly chopped
handful of parsley
2 Tbsp lentils
1 potato, scrubbed and diced

To make the stock, brown onions and shank (or beef shin) in a little bit of oil and then put in a larger pot. Cover with water and season lightly with salt and pepper. Add remaining stock ingredients and cook slowly on stove for at least 4 hours. Allow to cool overnight.

To make the soup, remove fat from top of stock. To the stock add the carrot, parsnip, onion, leek, parsley, lentils and potato. Boil slowly for a couple of hours until tender.

Check and adjust seasoning if necessary.

SERVES 10

My mother made Scotch Broth every week in the winter months. There was always a pot of shin bone, vegetables and pulses simmering on the stove. I used to wish we had tomato-heavy soups like minestrone, or thick leek and potato, basically anything other than this thin meat and vegetable essence. All these years later I have had quite enough of all those thick, blended, creamy and overly flavoured soups and I crave a good bowl of some of the exact soup made for us by Ian and Susie Todd.

SISI CIFUENTES HAILS FROM NICARAGUA, AND WHERE SHE COMES FROM MINCE IS CALLED GROUND STEAK. HER DISH IS A MORE SAVOURY MINCE THAN THE USUAL NEW ZEALAND VERSION. WITH CAPERS AND OLIVES, AND A GOOD DASH OF TABASCO, IT'S COOKED TO A DRIER, SISI SAYS 'CRUNCHY', CONSISTENCY.

Sisi's Mince Dish

Sisi was a good sport and served her mince on toast because we asked her to, but it really doesn't suit toast as much as it would rice.

olive oil for frying
1 onion, minced
1 tsp minced garlic
1 kg beef mince
1 Tbsp Worcestershire sauce
salt and pepper to taste
$\frac{1}{3}$ cup canned tomatoes
1 carrot, diced
1 potato, peeled and diced
8 baby corn cobs cut into chunks
$\frac{1}{2}$ cup beef stock
dash of Tabasco sauce
4 Tbsp mixed minced olives and capers

In a large pot, brown in olive oil the onion, garlic and mince. Add Worcestershire sauce. Mash it all together and add salt and pepper. Add remaining ingredients and cook until crunchy.

SERVES 4

Di's Apricot Sponge Pudding

    4 eggs, separated
    ³/₄ cup sugar
    100 g butter, melted
    1½–2 cups self-raising flour
    410 g can apricots

Preheat the oven to 150°C.
  Beat egg whites until stiff, add sugar gradually then add yolks and melted butter. Beat for only a minute. Fold in sifted flour (use a knife to mix).
  Place apricots in an ovenproof dish. Spoon sponge mixture over apricots. Cook in oven for about 45 minutes.

SERVES 4–6

It wasn't that long ago that pudding was served every night. It was usually hot and involved fruit, and if you didn't enjoy it you didn't deserve it but you had to eat it either way. There was far less obesity back when New Zealand families ate pudding. I am not sure that means that if everyone ate pudding every night the population would get slimmer, but if anyone wants to try I recommend they start with Di Gilchrist's Apricot Sponge Pudding.

Richard's All-Mince Meal

This is a menu for mince lovers. I'm not sure anyone should regularly eat menus with more than one course of mince, and the mince on toast and the hamburger recipes can quite cheerfully hold up almost any occasion on their own, but I would commend serious thought to the idea of hosting a Mince Party at least once in your life. Much like a fancy dessert, you've earned it. Expand it beyond these recipes, invite all your pals and get them all to bring a mince dish.

Central Otago Minestrone or Mince on Toast

I like my mince on toast quite tomato-y, and good and runny, or wet, or whatever you want to call it. Doubtless it sounds awful. The point of the wetness is to get a good level of sogginess into the bread onto which the reheated-the-next-day mince will be ladled.

50 g butter
3 onions, chopped
500 g beef mince
2 carrots, grated
1½ tsp dried oregano
3 dessertspoons tomato paste
2–2½ cups water (or stock)
salt and pepper to taste
2 cloves garlic, peeled and finely chopped
toast to serve

Melt butter in a good-sized saucepan over a medium-high heat. Add onion and soften. Add mince and stir to break up mince and allow it to brown lightly.

Add carrot, oregano, tomato paste and water or stock. Season to taste. Cover and turn down to a low simmer for an hour.

Allow to cool and reheat with chopped garlic before checking seasoning and serving on toast.

SERVES 4-6

IF YOU WERE TO BUY A GOOD WHITE LOAF, UNSLICED, AND WERE TO CUT THICKER THAN USUAL SLICES, TOAST THEM, BUTTER THEM AND THEN SMOTHER THEM IN MINCE, YOU WOULD BE REACHING A HIGHER PLANE IN PLAIN.

Kiwi Kitchen Burger Patties

Form these burger patties a bit on the plump side, cook them on the barbecue hot plate, get all the buns and fillings ready and you have a very simple and sleeve-staining party.

4 thick slices white bread
1 onion, roughly chopped
500 g beef mince
2 Tbsp tomato sauce
1 tsp mustard powder
2 tsp salt
freshly ground black pepper to taste
3 Tbsp red wine
oil for frying

In a food processor pulse together bread and onion until coarsely combined. In a large bowl combine this mixture with the next six ingredients.

When ready to make hamburgers, shape into patties and cook on a hot plate or in a frying pan.

Assemble with all the things you like to have in your burger. My list for a burger party would include:

chow chow relish
shredded iceberg lettuce
onion rings
  (soaked in water to
  soften onion blast)
sliced beetroot
sliced cheese
fried egg
tomato sauce
mayonnaise

SERVES 8–10

THE HAMBURGER IS ONE OF THE MOST REMARKABLE FOOD ITEMS. EVEN BAD ONES TASTE GOOD. BUT A GOOD ONE, COOKED THICK AND HEARTY AND LOADED WITH BEETROOT, IS THE COMPLETE KIWI EXPERIENCE.

Leila's Apricot Balls

Not all dried apricots are created equal. I seek the harder, more dried-out apricot halves, which are often a darker orange than the softer textured ones.

  1 cup dried apricots
  1 cup desiccated coconut
  ¼ cup sweetened condensed milk
  ¼ cup caster sugar

Mince apricots into a bowl. Add coconut and sweetened condensed milk and combine. Roll mixture into walnut-sized balls. Roll the balls in caster sugar and refrigerate.
  I keep them in the refrigerator in a glass jar with a screw-top lid.

MAKES 20-30

MY MOTHER USED TO
SERVE MINCED APRICOT
BALLS WITH COFFEE AT
SUPPER PARTIES. IT WOULD
HAVE TO BE A SUPPER
PARTY OF THE HIGHEST
ORDER. I LOVED TO HELP
BECAUSE I GOT TO PICK
THE BITS OF DRIED APRICOT
FROM THE STEEL PLATES
OF THE MINCER. I SAY HELP,
BUT I REALLY JUST HUNG
AROUND AND LOOKED
HOPEFUL AND HUNGRY. TO
THIS DAY, DRIED APRICOTS
ARE BETTER THAN CANDY
FOR ME.

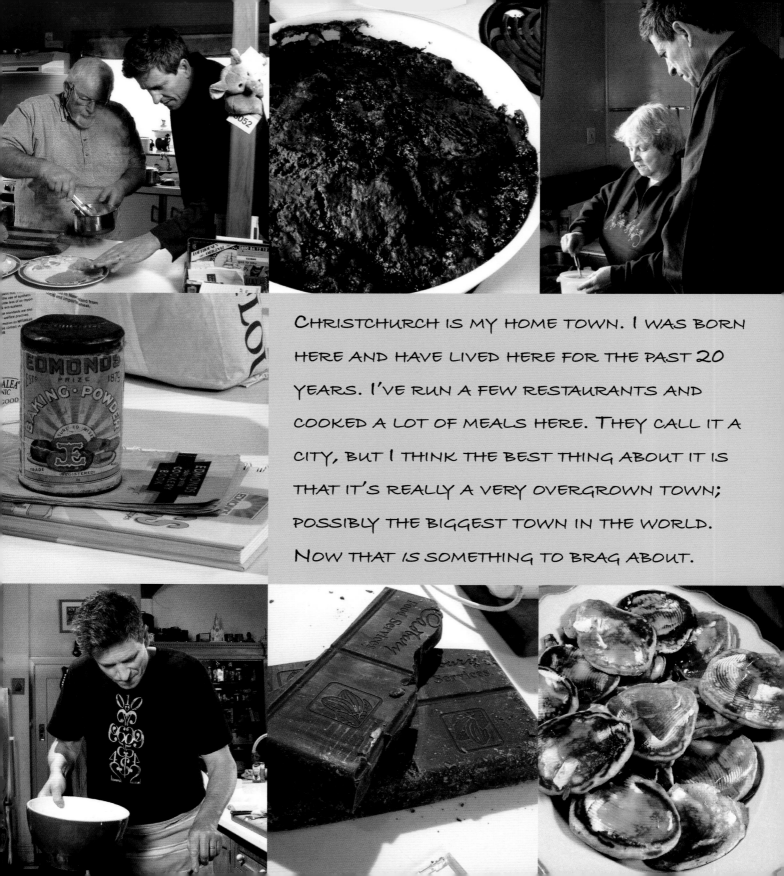

CHRISTCHURCH IS MY HOME TOWN. I WAS BORN HERE AND HAVE LIVED HERE FOR THE PAST 20 YEARS. I'VE RUN A FEW RESTAURANTS AND COOKED A LOT OF MEALS HERE. THEY CALL IT A CITY, BUT I THINK THE BEST THING ABOUT IT IS THAT IT'S REALLY A VERY OVERGROWN TOWN; POSSIBLY THE BIGGEST TOWN IN THE WORLD. NOW THAT IS SOMETHING TO BRAG ABOUT.

Home Town Favourites
Christchurch

Eventually it had to happen. An episode where I didn't get to go somewhere. I love eating and cooking, and I love travelling around New Zealand doing both of these things and talking about it. But it would be wrong to ignore Christchurch just because I live there.

Scones are probably made, or should I say 'whipped up' less often now than when I was a child. My mother whipped up scones. I have always loved a cheese scone best of all. They are the real scone in my mind. The reheated café cheese scone has never been nor will ever be as good a rendition as a batch 'whipped up' at home and served straight from the oven. For that's when they are at their best.

Corned beef was not my favourite meal when I was a child. Not really because of the meat; it was the vegetables boiled in the pot with the meat. The somewhat overcooked carrots held little appeal, but the real horror for me was the boiled parsnip. I have never warmed to boiled parsnip. Love it roasted, love it deep-fried, just don't expect me to be pleased with a plate of boiled parsnips.

What's not to like about a chocolate self-saucing pudding. You can buy packet mixes, you can even buy them canned and ready to heat and eat, but a home-made pudding is a really deceptively cheap and easy dish to knock together. Nothing could be nicer on a cold winter's evening.

Marg's Cheese Scones

The 'can of lemonade' scone recipe is the stuff of legend. But I'd never witnessed its production until we visited Marg Wright on the farm in Waikari in North Canterbury. Marg says it's quick to make and watching her in action it's hard to disagree.

4½ cups flour
4 tsp cream of tartar
2 tsp baking soda
2 cups grated tasty cheese
300 ml cream
330 ml can lemonade

Preheat the oven to 220°C.
  Sift dry ingredients together. Stir in grated cheese. Pour in cream and lemonade and just combine.
  Pat out into a rectangle and cut into smaller squares. Bake for 20 minutes or until golden.

MAKES 12–15

THERE WAS A TIME WHEN SCONES WERE WHIPPED UP LEFT, RIGHT AND CENTRE. MOTHERS WOULD PRODUCE HOT SCONES WITHOUT WARNING IN THE MIDDLE OF THE AFTERNOON. SOMETIMES TO COINCIDE WITH THE ARRIVAL OF RELATIVES OR OTHER FORMS OF VISITOR, BUT ALSO RANDOMLY. THEY ALWAYS APPEARED ON A WAVE OF BROWNED FLOUR AND BUTTER AROMA, WITH BUTTER AND JAM. SOMETIMES, BEST OF ALL, THEY WERE CHEESE SCONES.

Geff's Corned Beef Silverside

Geff Williamson is an older bachelor butcher in Christchurch. He serves his silverside with mashed potatoes, carrots with a little bit of orange zest, and finely sliced cabbage cooked with butter.

1 onion or leek, roughly chopped
1 carrot, roughly chopped
1 celery stalk, roughly chopped
1 corned beef silverside
1 Tbsp mustard powder
1 Tbsp manuka honey
2 tsp black peppercorns
3 bay leaves (fresh or dried)
water to cover corned beef
mustard sauce (see recipe opposite)

Place onion, carrot and celery in the bottom of a casserole pot or slow cooker. Place corned silverside on chopped vegetables. Sprinkle mustard powder on top and add manuka honey, peppercorns and bay leaves. Cover the whole lot with cold water. Put a tight-fitting lid on the casserole pot or slow cooker.

If cooking in a casserole pot, bring slowly to the boil on the stove top. Reduce heat to very low and allow to simmer for 3–4 hours, depending on the size of the corned silverside.

If cooking in a slow cooker, the cooking time will be at least 6 hours.

Remove from cooking liquid and dish it up with mustard sauce.

SERVES 6

Mustard Sauce

50 g butter
2 Tbsp flour
1 cup milk
1 Tbsp Dijon
   mustard
salt and pepper
   to taste

Heat butter in a
saucepan and add
the flour. Cook
until frothy. Stir
milk in slowly to
make a smooth
sauce. Simmer for
1 minute, stirring
constantly. Add
mustard and season
well.

CORNED SILVERSIDE, PRESERVED IN BRINE, IS A SOLID AND
ECONOMICAL WAY TO SERVE BEEF. WE VISITED A BUTCHER'S
SHOP IN EDGEWARE AND FOUND OUT HOW TECHNOLOGY HAS
ACCELERATED THE PROCESS OF CORNING BEEF FROM 9 WEEKS
TO 2 MINUTES, WITH THRUSTING NEEDLES SQUIRTING BRINE
UNDER EXTREME PRESSURE.

Aroha's Self-Saucing Chocolate Pudding

This is a super-cheap, super-easy, super-successful hot chocolate pudding.

60 g butter
½ cup self-raising flour
½ cup caster sugar
¼ cup cocoa
¾ cup milk
1 tsp vanilla essence
1 cup packed brown sugar
⅓ cup cocoa
2 cups boiling water

Preheat the oven to 180°C.

Melt butter and stir in flour, caster sugar, first measure of cocoa, milk and vanilla essence. Beat until smooth. Put mixture in an ovenproof dish.

Scatter brown sugar and second measure of cocoa over the batter in the dish and gently pour boiling water over the top.

Cook in the oven for 40 minutes.

SERVES 4

THE SUPERGRANS ARE
A BUNCH OF LEGENDS,
VOLUNTEERS WHO
PASS ON THEIR SKILLS
TO YOUNG PEOPLE,
PREDOMINANTLY WOMEN,
WHO ARE KEEN TO TAKE
MATTERS OF DOMESTICITY
INTO THEIR OWN HANDS.
GARDENING, COOKING
AND MENTORING. AROHA
WELLS, ONE OF THE
SUPERGRANS, RADIATES
AS MUCH WARMTH AS A
GOOD PUDDING AND SHE
MADE AN EXCEPTIONAL
CHOCOLATE SELF-SAUCING
ONE FOR US.

Richard's Brunch Menu

When New Zealanders discovered brunch in the 1980s, suddenly everyone had wait for their breakfast, then eat lots of rich food and drink sparkling wine mixed with orange juice with all the pulpy bits clinging to the glass. That was the 1980s. No-one actually drinks bucks fizz any more. But brunch carries bravely on.

Pikelets

2 Tbsp sugar
1 egg
1 scant cup milk
1½ cups flour, sifted
1½ tsp cream of tartar
½ tsp baking soda
1 Tbsp hot water
1 Tbsp butter, melted
pinch of salt

Beat sugar and egg together until light and frothy. Mix in milk, then flour, cream of tartar and baking soda. Mix together hot water, melted butter and salt. Stir into batter gently – as much as needed but no more.

Cook in batches, dropping spoonfuls of batter onto a lightly greased hot surface. Turn once as bubbles appear on the uncooked surface.

Keep on a plate covered with a tea towel until ready to serve.

MAKES 15

LONG BEFORE BRUNCH WAS CONCEIVED, MORNING TEA RULED. BRUNCH IS A SORT OF DRIFTING MEAL BUT MORNING TEA NEATLY BISECTS THE GAP BETWEEN BREAKFAST AND LUNCH. I'M BRINGING THE MORNING TEA INTO BRUNCH BY SUGGESTING YOU MAKE PIKELETS.

Corned Beef Hash

You can make the basic hash mixture a day ahead and crisp it up in a frying pan, on a barbecue hot plate or, best of all, in your toasted sandwich maker.

25 g butter for frying
2 onions, chopped
10 potatoes, cubed and boiled until tender
1 kg corned beef silverside, cooked for 4 hours and cubed
1 tsp chopped fresh thyme
¹⁄₃ cup cream
salt and pepper to taste

Heat a large skillet or frypan. Add butter and onion, potato and corned beef. Cook, covered, for 30 minutes over a medium-low heat, turning frequently with a firm spatula or fish slice. Make sure you turn it carefully, getting all the browning material off the bottom of the pan. It browns slowly at first and more quickly over time.

Add thyme, cream, and salt and pepper. Cover and cook for a further 30 minutes, scraping and turning every few minutes.

SERVES 6-8

CORNED BEEF HASH IS NOT A VERY KIWI DISH. BUT IT'S DELICIOUS AND IT USES CORNED SILVERSIDE. I LEARNT HOW TO MAKE IT FROM A JULIA CHILD VIDEO. IT IS A RICH DISH. YOU WON'T FIND IT ON ANY CARDIAC CARE RECIPE LEAFLETS.

Hollandaise Sauce

This recipe is for the minimum amount I've had success with in a regular-sized food processor bowl. The three yolks will take double the amount of butter listed in the recipe, but it's hard to get the emulsion under way with less than three yolks. If you have one of those dinky little food processors, maybe it's possible to make smaller volumes, but I can't tell you.

250 g butter
3 egg yolks
juice of ½ a lemon
   (or lime)

Melt the butter and keep it hot. Put the yolks and juice in the food processor bowl and set it running. Allow processor to run for 20 seconds. With the motor still running, add the butter, very slowly at first, slightly faster as the emulsion begins to form, and faster still as the volume grows. Turn the processor off as soon as you have added all the butter.

MAKES APPROXIMATELY 2 CUPS

THE CORNERSTONE OF THE BRUNCH CONCEPT IS HOLLANDAISE SAUCE – IT'S THE KEY INGREDIENT IN EGGS BENEDICT, AND A GOOD FRIEND OF MOST SAVOURY BREAKFAST AND LUNCH DISHES. IT'S OFTEN SEEN AS BEING TRICKY, BUT IT'S EASY TO MAKE IN THE FOOD PROCESSOR IF YOU ARE MAKING ENOUGH OF IT. AFTER SLOW BRUNCH SHIFTS IN RESTAURANTS THERE WOULD OFTEN BE A HALF LITRE OF HOLLANDAISE LEFT OVER. ON THOSE DAYS I USED TO SEE HOW LITTLE MONEY WOULD CONVINCE A DISHWASHER TO DRINK IT. TERRIBLE PLACES, RESTAURANT KITCHENS.

When you are travelling you still have to eat. It might mean stopping at a roadside café for coffee and a snack, having a pie in a pub or even just sucking an Air New Zealand lolly, it's all travelling food. It gives you something to look forward to and gives you a chance to eat things you mightn't cook for yourself.

Travellers' Fare
Planes, Boats and Trains

THERE'S OFTEN A SPECIAL GOLDEN GLOW AROUND OUR MEMORIES OF FAMILY
HOLIDAYS. BATHED IN THIS AURA, MANY OTHERWISE ORDINARY MEALS SHINE IN
THE IMAGINATION. MY OWN MEMORIES OF SAUSAGES BOILED IN MAGGI SPRING
VEGETABLE SOUP MIX THICKENED AT THE LAST MOMENT WITH INSTANT MASHED
POTATO FLAKES ARE AKIN TO THE LEGENDS OF AMBROSIA. I'M ALMOST CERTAIN
THAT ANY ATTEMPT TO REPRODUCE THE MEAL WOULD EXPOSE ITS SHORTCOMINGS.
THE MEAL WAS MADE BY ITS CONTEXT RATHER THAN THE INGREDIENTS OR
METHOD.

I HAVE MANY MEMORIES OF HOLIDAY MEALS AND ALMOST AS MANY OF MEALS
WHILE TRAVELLING TO THE HOLIDAY DESTINATION. ROADSIDE TAKEAWAYS ON A
LONG CAR JOURNEY STAND OUT, AS DOES THE EXPERIENCE OF DRIVING THROUGH
SMALL TOWN AFTER SMALL TOWN ON A FRIDAY EVENING AND GETTING A WHIFF OF
FISH AND CHIPS IN EVERY ONE OF THEM.

I DON'T HAVE ANY RECOLLECTION OF RAIL TRAVEL IN THE DAYS OF THE RAILWAY
TEAROOMS, BUT THEY COULD TEACH US A THING OR TWO ABOUT CAFÉ SERVICE.
IN 1946 THE RAILWAYS TEAROOMS SERVED 9 MILLION CUSTOMERS BY THE
TRAINLOAD IN BURSTS OF FOUR MINUTES. THE PASSENGERS WOULD CROWD
FIVE DEEP AT THE COUNTER FOR TEA, PIE AND BAKING. THE WOMEN IN THOSE
TEAROOMS SERVED 20 PEOPLE IN THE TIME IT TAKES ONE OF OUR MODERN
BARISTAS TO FASHION A FERN PATTERN IN THE CREMA.

Margaret's Sugar Buns

110 g butter
2 cups flour
¾ cup sugar
2 tsp baking powder
1 cup sultanas
2 eggs
milk to make up to 1 cup
jam for tops
sugar for sprinkling

Preheat the oven to 180°C.
  In a food processor,
combine butter, flour,
sugar and baking powder
and whizz. Add sultanas.
  Put eggs in a tea cup
and fill up with milk. Tip
into a separate bowl and
beat with egg beater.
  Mix liquids into dry
ingredients and put in
spoonfuls on greased tray.
  Carefully spoon 1 tsp
jam onto the top of each
blob of mixture. Sprinkle
sugar over and bake for
10–12 minutes.

MAKES 16

MARGARET HISLOP
HAS MANY MEMORIES
OF TRAIN TRAVEL FROM
HER CHILDHOOD AND
SHE MADE A SLIGHTLY
MODERNISED VERSION
OF A SUGAR BUN
THAT SHE STRONGLY
ASSOCIATES WITH THE
RAIL TRAVEL OF HER
YOUTH.

I HAVE A VIVID RECOLLECTION OF THE FOOD ON THE COOK STRAIT FERRIES, AND IT IS NOT GOOD. I CANNOT ERASE FROM MY MEMORY A PIE I ATE DURING THE LONG SMOOTH PASSAGE THROUGH THE MARLBOROUGH SOUNDS. IT WASN'T SO MUCH THE PIE AS THE GRAVY IT WAS SERVED WITH. I SWEAR IT WAS WATERY MARMITE. I LOVE MARMITE WHEN IT'S SPARINGLY SMEARED ON TOAST, EVEN ON A SPLIT SAVELOY, BUT NOT THICK AND STRONG, AND CERTAINLY NOT STRONG BUT WATERY AROUND A PIE.

Dave's Crumbed Dory with Chips

On the ferry *Kaitaki* I was welcomed into the ship's galley by Dave Lawson. He showed us crumbed fish and chips and frightened me with stories of deep fryers in heavy seas and the joys of dodging boiling oil.

    fresh or frozen dory
    egg yolk
    dry breadcrumbs
    potatoes
    oil for deep frying

Cover dory in egg yolk and then coat with breadcrumbs. Deep fry for 3-4 minutes.
  Cut potatoes into chips and deep fry.
  Serve crumbed dory and chips with a fresh salad.

DESPITE EACH EXPERIENCE OF ECONOMY CLASS AIRLINE FOOD, I STILL LOOK FORWARD TO THE NEXT MEAL. I NEVER MANAGE TO EAT THEM WITH ANY GUSTO, BUT IT NEVER IMPACTS ON THE EXCITEMENT AND ANTICIPATION OF ANOTHER AIRLINE MEAL. ON THOSE LONG-HAUL FLIGHTS IT'S AS MUCH ABOUT BOREDOM RELIEF AS IT IS THE INEXPLICABLE PLEASURES OF LITTLE CONTAINERS OF DIFFERENT FOODS ON A LITTLE TRAY, WITH EVERYTHING SEALED IN IMPENETRABLE PLASTIC WRAPPING.

I HAD THE GREAT PLEASURE OF DESIGNING MEALS FOR AIR NEW ZEALAND DOMESTIC SERVICE IN THE 1990s. AT THE HEIGHT OF THE ANSETT VERSUS AIR NEW ZEALAND SERVICE WAR THAT ULTIMATELY ENDED WITH COMMON SENSE RULING THE DAY, AND ALL MEALS DISAPPEARING ON DOMESTIC SERVICE. THE REMNANTS, A TUB OF WATER AND A HANDFUL OF BOILED SWEETS, ARE SEEN BY SOME AS MERELY GIVING THE FLIGHT ATTENDANTS SOMETHING TO DO IN BETWEEN ATTENDING TO THE SAFETY REQUIREMENTS OF PASSENGER MANAGEMENT IN COMMERCIAL AVIATION. I LOVE THE BOILED LOLLIES TOO MUCH TO SHARE THAT VIEW. IT'S ONE OF THE GREAT REMNANTS OF THE OLD DAYS IN TRAVEL.

OUR GUESTS NAOMI ROUNTREE AND ANN GRIEVE WERE BOTH FLIGHT ATTENDANTS WITH AIR NEW ZEALAND IN THE DAYS WHEN THEY WERE KNOWN AS AIR HOSTESSES. THEY HAD WITNESSED AT FIRST HAND THE JOURNEY OF DOMESTIC AIRLINE CATERING FROM THE DAYS OF A LITTLE CARDBOARD BOX WITH A SANDWICH AND A PIECE OF FRUIT, THROUGH THE CHEESE AND CRACKERS IN PLASTIC WRAPPERS THAT PROVIDED AN HOUR'S ENTERTAINMENT TO PASSENGERS WHO FOOLISHLY TRIED TO OPEN THEM, TO THE DAYS OF THE FULL-SERVICE MEALS ON ALL MAIN TRUNK ROUTES INCLUDING THE 25-MINUTE FLIGHT BETWEEN WELLINGTON AND CHRISTCHURCH. CRAZY DAYS INDEED.

Richard's On-the-Move Menu

My away from home menu is designed for cooking on limited equipment, camping, in a tent or caravan. My own ideal scenario for this is the caravan, particularly in a caravan on a blustery, cold, rainy night, the sound of rain drumming on the roof, inches from your head, the little stove struggling away trying to cook a meal for happy campers. They'll remain happy as long as the meal is good, and the rain stops by morning.

Campfire Potatoes

10 large potatoes
water to cover
1½ tsp salt
2 cubes vegetable stock
4 Tbsp cream
2 Tbsp butter
instant mashed potato flakes to thicken
pepper to taste

Peel (or not) and roughly cube potatoes. Barely cover with water. Add salt. Cover and simmer until cooked. To undrained potatoes add stock cubes, cream and butter and chop together like a potato salad. If there is still water slopping about, add instant mashed potato flakes until liquid is absorbed. Add pepper, check and adjust seasoning if necessary.

SERVES 6

CAMPFIRE POTATOES WAS AN EXPERIMENTAL DISH THAT WITH THE FIRST BITE WON THE HEARTS OF MY VERY TIRED AND VERY HUNGRY SONS ON A TRAMPING EXPEDITION. IT'S POSSIBLE THE VERY TIRED AND VERY HUNGRY PARTS ARE KEY INGREDIENTS, SO DO NOT TRY THIS AT HOME.

Beef Olives

Making these small beef olives is a sort of handcraft therapy, and the result is sure to delight your diners. Especially if you turn it out in extremis, in the middle of nowhere, on a barbecue.

1 packet stuffing mix
1 red onion, finely chopped
8 pieces beef schnitzel
flour seasoned with salt and pepper
olive oil for frying
1 onion, chopped
1 carrot, finely diced
20 small button mushrooms
half bottle of red wine
1 x 400 g can chopped tomatoes
2 Tbsp dried oregano
1 tsp paprika
water or stock to cover
salt and pepper to taste

Make stuffing according to the manufacturer's instructions and add red onion.

Cut schnitzel into long, vaguely triangular pieces. Mostly you'll get two out of a piece, but sometimes they are huge and you'll get more.

Take lumps of stuffing and roll the meat around them. Start at the bottom of the meat isosceles and roll to the tip. Set aside and repeat until you have a nice little pile of these smaller than usual beef olives.

When they are all made, dust with well-seasoned flour and brown lightly in batches, in oil, in a frypan or on a barbecue hot plate. As they become browned, add them to a large pot.

If you are using a frypan, soften the second chopped onion, the carrot and button mushrooms in the pan. Deglaze the pan with wine and tip the whole lot into the pot with the beef olives.

If you are using a barbecue hotplate, just add the onion, carrot and mushroom with the wine directly into the large pot without frying first.

Add tomatoes, oregano, paprika and water or stock to just cover, if the wine and tomatoes don't. Season with salt and pepper. Simmer on the stovetop for 1–2 hours.

SERVES 6–8

THE BEEF OLIVES MY MOTHER
USED TO BUY FROM THE BUTCHER
WERE SO LARGE WE GOT ONLY ONE
EACH FOR DINNER. I REMEMBER
THE STUFFING WITH ITS SHARP
SPEARS OF DRIED ROSEMARY
THREATENING TO PUNCTURE THE
ROOF OF YOUR MOUTH, THE WAY
THE BEEF OLIVES AT THE TOP OF
THE DISH GOT A LITTLE BIT CRISPY
ALONG THE SIDE THAT STUCK
OUT OF THE GRAVY, AND HOW I
IMAGINED THEY MUST BE DIFFICULT
TO MAKE. THEY ARE REALLY VERY
EASY TO MAKE AND I CAN SEE
NOW THAT THEY WERE A LITTLE
INTRUSION OF CONVENIENCE INTO
MY MOTHER'S ROUTINE, WHICH
JUST MAKES ME LIKE THEM MORE.

Campfire Bread and Butter Pudding

¼ cup sultanas
¼ cup old booze
4 eggs
2 Tbsp brown sugar
1 cup cream
½ cup flour
8 slices white bread
4 Tbsp jam

Soak sultanas in the old booze overnight.
  Beat together eggs, sugar and cream. Add flour and combine.
  Make bread and jam into sandwiches and cut into fine dice. Add to the batter, along with the boozy sultanas.
  Cook pikelet-size pancakes in a frypan or on hotplate. Serve hot.

MAKES 20

THIS CAMPING DESSERT IS A BIT OF A NOD TO DAMPER AND ALL THOSE FLOURY CAMPING PUDDINGS, AND IT MAKES FURTHER USE OF THE FLAT PLATE BARBECUE. IT SEEMS THAT ONE IS NEVER VERY FAR FROM ONE OF THOSE BARBECUES THESE DAYS. IT'S A BIT OF A PANCAKE, AND IT'S A BIT OF A BREAD AND BUTTER PUDDING AND IT'S AN OPPORTUNITY TO CLEAN OUT THE BOOZE CUPBOARD BY TIPPING STUFF FROM THE DUSTY OLD BOTTLES FROM THE BACK CORNER INTO SOME COOKING. EVERYTHING SEEMS FLASHER WITH A BIT OF BOOZE IN IT, ESPECIALLY ON LONG SUMMER CAMPING EVENINGS.

CHICKEN IS NEW ZEALAND'S FAVOURITE MEAT. TRY TALKING TO SOMEONE WHO HAS TRAVELLED SOMEWHERE EXOTIC AND EATEN SOMETHING ODD, PERHAPS ARMADILLO, OR CROCODILE, OR DOG, OR ... WELL, YOU GET THE IDEA. NINETY-NINE PERCENT OF THE TIME, WHEN ASKED WHAT IT TASTED LIKE, THAT PERSON WILL SAY 'IT TASTES LIKE CHICKEN'.

A Chicken Dinner
Taranaki

In the last episode of the second series of *Kiwi Kitchen* we went to Taranaki, where we finally tackled chicken, 'the bird', the most popular meat in New Zealand. To satisfy New Zealanders' hunger for chicken 88,214,000 birds are reared and slaughtered every year (as of 2004). That translates into each and every New Zealander eating 37.1 kg of chicken meat in the year.

This is a significant shift from my childhood in the 1960s, when a chicken meal was a rare luxury. Chickens came whole and generally speaking were roast. The smell of a chicken roasting is one of the great comforting, heart-warming smells of the kitchen.

The only problem with these joyous family celebrations is that supplying the meat we love at a price we love requires industrial poultry farming and the associated suffering of animals. I'm pleased to see there are increasing numbers of food producers selling us how they produce as much as what they produce. If we are prepared to pay a little extra, we can eat chicken without having to turn a blind eye to the abuse.

None of this makes the chicken taste any less delicious, of course. I know, I ate one last night.

Jamie's Fried Mushrooms

Surfing develops a good hunger. Jamie has a quick remedy for his hunger in the form of a stove-top fry-up. It features mushrooms on toast, a great dish indeed, and one that can come in many different forms and be totally delicious in totally different ways.

    mushrooms, sliced
    tomatoes, halved
    bacon
    bread
    parsley

Fry mushrooms and tomatoes. Grill bacon. Toast bread. Assemble mushrooms, tomatoes and bacon on toast. Garnish with parsley.

I associate Mt Taranaki with mushrooms. Special mushrooms. We visited Jamie Andrews, a champion surfer who cooked mushrooms on toast, with trimmings. Ordinary mushrooms, special guy. Jamie, his mushroom dish, his surfing, his partner and their baby together seemed to capture perfectly the spirit of small-town, 'live to surf' Taranaki.

I LIKE THE CUT OF ALI GIRLING-BUTCHER'S JIB. SHE ADMITS TO ALWAYS GIVING OUT HER RECIPE FOR LASAGNE WITH AN INGREDIENT MISSING. MANY OF US ARE GUILTY OF THIS IN ONE WAY OR ANOTHER. FROM BEING A BIT OBSCURE ABOUT THE METHOD, TO KNOWING FULL WELL THAT THE CHIPPED TEA CUP YOU USE IS CLOSER TO 3/4 CUP THAN A CUP. IT'S SOMETHING FROM THE MISCHIEVOUS SIDE OF HOSPITALITY, AND VERY HUMAN.

ALI'S WOOD-BURNING STOVE MADE ME FEEL VERY ENVIOUS. SOMETHING THAT WARMS THE HOUSE *AND* COOKS THE DINNER. I'D JUST LOVE TO BE STOKING THE FIRE THAT COOKED THE CASSEROLE; IT'S ANOTHER WAY TO FEEL INVOLVED WITH YOUR DINNER. SADLY, I DON'T THINK I'D BE ALLOWED ONE IN OUR HOUSE.

Ali's Chicken Casserole

This casserole has all the classic 'good with chicken' ingredients. Bacon, mushrooms, garlic, wine. We don't all have wood stoves to cook our casseroles in, as Ali does, but a good long slow cook in a regular domestic oven will do just as well.

6 chicken legs
flour for dusting
oil for frying
3 rashers smoky bacon
1 large leek, sliced
1 Tbsp chopped fresh lemon thyme
1 Tbsp chopped fresh marjoram
500 g button mushrooms, chopped
¾ cup white wine
2 tsp Dijon mustard
4 cloves garlic, peeled and crushed
zest and juice of 2 lemons
1 tsp Moroccan seasoning
½ cup water
salt and pepper to taste

Preheat the oven to 150°C.

Flour chicken legs and fry in oil. When browned nicely place in ovenproof casserole dish. Chop bacon and add to casserole.

Sweat leek in frypan then place in casserole along with lemon thyme and marjoram. Cook chopped mushrooms in frypan.

Deglaze the frypan by mixing in it wine, mustard, garlic, lemon zest and juice, Moroccan seasoning and water. Pour over the casserole. Season with salt and pepper.

Place casserole in oven and cook for about 2½ hours.

SERVES 4–6

Diane's Bread and Butter Pudding

1 loaf stale sliced bread (white bread or fruit bread)
butter for bread
apricot jam for bread
handful of sultanas
6 eggs
3 cups milk
1 tsp vanilla essence
½ cup sugar
¼ tsp ground cinnamon or grated nutmeg

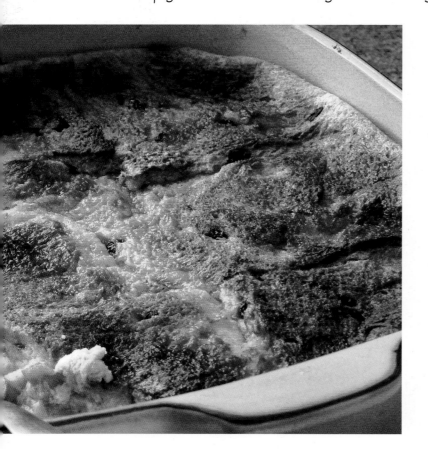

Preheat the oven to 180°C.

Butter bread and remove crusts. Place a layer of bread, buttered side down, in an ovenproof casserole dish. Lightly spread bread with jam. Sprinkle with sultanas. Build up in layers, finishing with a jam layer.

Lightly beat eggs, milk, vanilla and sugar and pour over bread. Top with a final layer of bread, buttered side up. Sprinkle with cinnamon or nutmeg.

Place dish in a roasting tin with boiling water coming three-quarters of the way up the side of the dish.

Cook in oven for 45 minutes or until golden and puffy.

SERVES 6

BREAD AND BUTTER PUDDING, MADE WITH RAISIN TOAST BREAD FROM THE YARROWS BAKERY JUST DOWN THE ROAD IN MANAIA, IS POPULAR FARE IN DIANE WINEERA'S HOUSE. SHE MAKES IT OFTEN, AND THIS SHOWS IN THE CONFIDENT WAY SHE THROWS IT TOGETHER. DIANE AND HER FAMILY REGULARLY HOST EXCHANGE STUDENTS FROM EVERY CORNER OF THE GLOBE. SHE SENDS THEM ALL HOME WITH A LOVE OF THE KIWI BREAD AND BUTTER PUDDING.

RICHARD'S CHICKEN IN A BASKET MEAL

Since more chicken meals are made around the country than pretty much any other kind, I thought I'd better chip in a recipe or two myself. After 16 episodes in the television programme without a chicken dish, it's time to take it on.

Richard's Mushrooms on Toast

These mushrooms make an excellent sauce for steak or roast beef, as well as being an entrée on toast, as it is for this menu.

50 g butter
½ cup flour
1 cup milk
1 tsp salt
1.5 kg flat mushrooms
pepper to taste
3 cloves garlic, peeled and
　finely chopped
bread for toasting
　(1 or 2 slices per diner)
butter for toast

Melt butter in a large saucepan. Add flour and stir over low heat for 2 minutes. Add milk and whisk together over a medium heat until mixture thickens. It will be very thick. Add salt.

Roughly chop, or crumble, the mushrooms into the white sauce and mix together. Cover, reduce heat to low and cook for 30 minutes, stirring frequently. The mushrooms will release a great deal of water and the mixture will become quite liquid.

Remove lid and cook for a further 20 minutes.

Add pepper, check seasoning and adjust if necessary. If possible, refrigerate overnight.

When ready to serve, reheat mushrooms, adding the finely chopped garlic. Serve on thick slices of buttered toast.

SERVES 6–10

I USED TO CLIMB THE HILLS OF THE OTAGO PENINSULA PICKING MUSHROOMS JUST SO MY MOTHER WOULD MAKE MUSHROOMS ON TOAST. WHEN SHE MADE IT WITH BIG 'HORSE' MUSHROOMS, THE RESULT WAS AS BLACK AS PITCH. I DON'T OFTEN HAVE FIELD MUSHROOMS THESE DAYS AND I MAKE THIS DISH WITH THE BIG FLAT MUSHROOMS FROM THE SUPERMARKET. IT'S NEVER BLACK AS PITCH, AND NEVER AS DARKLY MUSHROOMY IN FLAVOUR, BUT IT'S GOOD NEVERTHELESS.

Chicken in a Basket

4 eggs
¼ cup cream
1 Tbsp Dijon mustard
3 tsp salt
1 tsp white pepper
3 cloves garlic, peeled and finely minced
2 kg chicken pieces
2 cups fine dry breadcrumbs

Preheat the oven to 190°C.
  In a large bowl mix together eggs, cream, mustard, salt, pepper and garlic. Place chicken pieces in mixture and coat well.
  Put breadcrumbs in a clean supermarket bag. Add chicken pieces, well coated in egg mixture, two at a time to the supermarket bag and toss until chicken is coated with crumbs.
  Place on a well-oiled oven tray and cook in the oven for 45 minutes, turning once.

SERVES 8

CHICKEN IN A BASKET WAS AN AMAZING CONCEPT TO ME IN THE 1970s. IT WAS NOT LIKE I WENT TO RESTAURANTS MUCH, BUT I KNEW ABOUT THE BASIC TYPES OF MEAL. ROASTS, STEAKS, SPAGHETTI BOLOGNESE, SOUP, STEWS — ALL THINGS THAT CAME ON A PLATE OR IN A BOWL. NOW HERE WAS A MEAL THAT CAME IN A BASKET AND WAS CRUMBED. IT SAT OUTSIDE THE ORDINARY RULES OF DINNER AND WAS A BEACON OF MODERN LIVING.

Lemon Delicious

This is a masterpiece of kitchen chemistry and physics. It's a mixture that separates as it cooks, leaving a cake-y top and a runny lemony underneath. It's quick to throw together and it's a pudding everyone will love.

    50 g butter
    1 cup sugar
    zest and juice of 1 lemon
    2 Tbsp flour
    2 eggs, separated
    1 cup milk

Preheat the oven to 160°C.

Cream the butter and sugar together. Add the lemon zest and juice. Stir in flour and egg yolks. Add milk and combine.

In a separate bowl beat egg whites until stiff. Fold the egg whites into batter. Place mixture in a pudding dish. Put the dish inside a roasting tin with water half way up the sides of the dish.

Cook in the oven for 1 hour.

SERVES 6

LEMON DELICIOUS IS A CLASSIC KIWI PUDDING. AND I OFFER YOU A VERSION OF THE RECIPE PUBLISHED BY TUI FLOWER, HERSELF A KIWI CLASSIC. SHE TRAINED IN PARIS A FEW YEARS BEFORE JULIA CHILD DID, AND IS BEST KNOWN AS THE ONE-TIME FOOD EDITOR FOR THE *NEW ZEALAND WOMEN'S WEEKLY*. SHE HAS SOUND CLASSICAL TECHNIQUE AND A GREAT RESPECT FOR METHOD. AND SHE'S NOT SHORT OF AN OPINION.

Recipe Index